TRANSFORMATIONAL LEADERSHIP IN EDUCATION

STRENGTHS-BASED APPROACH TO CHANGE FOR ADMINISTRATORS, TEACHERS, AND GUIDANCE COUNSELORS

Hollis L. Green, ThD, PhD

GlobalEdAdvancePress™

TRANSFORMATIONAL LEADERSHIP IN EDUCATION

Copyright © 2010 by Hollis L. Green

Library of Congress Control Number: 2010923272

Green, Hollis L., 1933 –
        Transformational Leadership in Education:
        Strengths-based Approach to Change for Administrators,
        Teachers and Guidance Counselors

        ISBN 978-0-9801674-6-7

        Subject Codes and Description:
        1: EDU.000000: Education: General 2; EDU032000. Education:
        Leadership 3; EDU 040000. Education: Philosophy & Social Aspects

Cover Design by Barton Green

Published by
GlobalEdAdvancePress
www.globaledadvance.org

WITH GRATITUDE TO ALL WHO
VALUED LEARNING AND TAUGHT ME
THE EXCITEMENT OF DISCOVERY,

THIS BOOK IS RESPECTFULLY DEDICATED
IN MEMORY OF

LELA HUDSON HOODENPYLE
(1912 - 1983)

WHO POINTED ME TOWARD
LIFE LONG LEARNING.

Hollis L. Green, BA(BS), BD, MEd, ThD, PhD

TABLE OF CONTENTS

Introduction

Education and Life Applications

Framework for Viewing Classroom Learning

Individuals approach the teaching/learning process with relatively fixed attitudes. This predisposition was shaped by the early stages of knowledge base formation. Since learning about the unknown is directly related to the known, those students with weak foundations may turn into **reluctant** or **obstinate** learners and become indirectly influenced by peers more than the direct influence of the teacher. Managing their conduct normally will cause the teaching/learning process to be more difficult. **Such students may need extra tutoring and personal attention.** Family and community environment and mature attitudes about education influence this predisposition. Bonding with mature students and personality development are factors that assist in the formation of these learning attitudes.

CLASSIFICATION OF LEARNING ATTITUDES

Excellent Learners	Informal Learners	Reluctant Learners	Obstinate Learners
Have a strong desire to learn	Require a more relaxed, less structured process	Are cautious about participating, but will follow the crowd	Are unwilling to change and difficult to manage

Figure 0.1 –Student Attitudes or Predisposition to Learn.

Normal healthy age-specific development together with positive influence from family and friends will produce an **excellent** student who desires to learn. Teaching such students is almost effortless because they are self-starters. The development of certain personality traits and individual characteristics may produce an **informal** learner who requires a more relaxed and less structured process, for learning. Such students may see things differently than others and develop study and work habits that may not fit the norm. In reality, these may not receive the highest grades in the class, but they may actually be the better learners with long-term benefits that predict personal and professional achievements.

In some educational systems, the informal learner may be classified as a "C" student but will probably end up owning the business and hiring the excellent students to do the work. A list in history may verify this possibility. Some of the informal learners that ended up on top of the heap were Edison, Lincoln, Einstein, von Braun, Reagan, Kennedy, Clinton, Bush, and the list goes on and on.

Opportunity Equals Obligation

Although many students are reluctant learners, all students have motives for their action. The task of the teacher is to understand these motives and provide an activity to assist the student toward their desired goals. Parents and family can assist, but the last-ditch stand is in the classroom. Teachers must be aware of what activates the motive of students to learn. Each opportunity is an obligation for the teacher. The classroom can change the world one student at a time. It is a privilege to be trusted as a teacher.

As a preschooler, Albert Einstein was sick in bed when his father gave him a compass. Einstein later recalled the excitement and wonder as he examined the mysterious powers of the compass. The needle seemed to move as if influenced by a distant force. There were no mechanical explanation for the moves and young Einstein perceived that some deep mystery was behind the movement of the compass hand. This curiosity led to Einstein's thinking about magnetic fields, gravity, inertia and light beams and gave him a life direction.

An uncle who was an engineer introduced young Albert to algebra calling it a "merry science." By age thirteen Einstein exhibited a predisposition for solving complicated problems in the field of applied mathematics. Writing an essay on theoretical physics at age 16, Einstein was well on his way to discovering the Theory of Relativity. The record shows that Einstein had difficulty with ordinary math and may not have received the necessary encouragement from teachers, but by age 40 Albert Einstein's life applications would make him world famous. His journey toward greatness began as a sick preschooler studying the hands of a compass. This thoughtful gift from a sensitive parent and the later academic encouragement from an uncle produced an individual who changed the world. This also points to the joint influence of family members and teachers in intellectual achievements.

A human element behind today's satellite and space exploits, Wernher von Braun, became interested in space as a small boy. This German-born scientist saw a drawing of a rocket streaking through space and sent for the booklet. The illustration caught the interest of young von Braun, but he was startled to find the booklet contained mostly sophisticated mathematical equations. Young von Braun disliked math and had difficulty with the subject in school, but this fact did not discourage this young scientist to be. His interest had been sparked, he had formalized a motive and a vehicle was discovered to facilitate his ultimate goal and his life-objective. He was interested in space, so some teacher unlocked the secrets and used his childhood memories to apply math solutions to his life-application. To learn more about space, he had to study math. With the encouragement of others, he made the choice, "If I must know math to learn about space then I will learn math." His motive to learn about space using the activity of improving math skills, even in spite of the struggles of War, he became the personification of man's struggle to rise above his environment and reach for higher goals. His life struggle and life applications still benefit the world.

The youthful dreams of many achieving individuals have provided a worthy life-direction. Abraham Lincoln's lofty ambitions were born as he counted the stars through the cracks in a cabin roof. Hard work and a difficult personal struggle for an adequate education developed basic gifts for debate and decision. With limited light from an open fireplace, Lincoln pressed the envelope of learning until he rose to the highest office in America and literally stabilized the future of the United States of America by confronting division, slavery, and injustice, and preserved a union that became a force for good in the world.

Thomas A. Edison describing his systematic and detailed life said, "I never did anything worth doing by accident." His intentionality produced hopes and dreams and materialized because he possessed and used untiringly a great inventive talent. In addition to perseverance, the real secret to Edison's achievements was that he saw all failure and disappointment as a learning experience and found a way to turn the negative aspects of his life and work into positive adventures.

All individuals desiring to be called "teacher" to be adequate to the task must learn this lesson and deal with negativity in a positive manner. This illustrates a basic rule in philosophy; one can never reach a positive conclusion beginning with a negative premise. A second construct of philosophy is appropriate here: a positive implies a negative. When a positive life-direction is determined there is confidence that much of the negativity of life can be avoided by applying the positive influence of parents and teachers.

Transformational Teachers

A clear need for methodology suggests that a learning leader may be needed. When a process appears to be complicated, it may only be sophisticated and a teacher or instructor may direct the learner on a path through the maze. Once the footsteps are on the guided path, the process is no longer complicated and the learner can move forward with limited guidance. Teachers then become facilitators of learning.

Transformational teachers must conceptualize their roles significantly more than the classroom monitor, current learning leaders in the classroom, tutoring positions, and guidance counselors must become computer instructors, technology users and Internet surfers and not only talkers, chalkboard or whiteboard writers. Listening also advances the teaching/ learning process. Teachers become facilitators in the process of self-directed learning. The tutors and classroom teachers operate as consultants; provide referrals and resources for the learner. The learning leader, regardless of the title, must establish an environment which encourages self-diagnosis, the formulation of objectives and the learner's ability for the design, implementation and continuation of learning strategies.

Twenty-first century learning leaders must be aware of the problems in a non-conventional educational environment and must be aware and utilize the available technology to enhance the learning experience. They need to be knowledgeable of the learner's physical, psychological, social, cultural and family environment and function in an appropriate manner to enhance an atmosphere conducive to self-directed learning. The teaching and learning philosophy and subsequent teaching style obviously form crucial elements in appropriate interface with self-directed learners. From a philosophical point of view, both pragmatism and existentialism seem least at odds with self-directed learning. The former has obvious advantages with its emphasis on experiential reality and the latter because of its basis on reality as existence (Gutek 1988).

In ancient sacred writings there was a follower of a Master Teacher who measured his life-purpose and achievements by articulating a controlling principle of his life, "This one thing I do...reaching forth for those things which are before." The positive reaching forward caused him to forget the negative things of the past. This was the focus of Saul of Tarsus on pleasing the Master Teacher and doing good for mankind that gave his life courage to overcome difficulties and confidence to face the future. He wrote to a young teacher, "And entrust the things you learned from me which were confirmed by many witnesses, to faithful men who will be competent to teach others also. (2 Timothy 2:2 DNT) In the view of this teacher, the teaching profession was a perpetual assembly line turning out competent learners who were capable of becoming knowledgeable teachers.

Necessity and Possibility

Classroom leaders and the educational delivery system relate to modalities and mechanisms that include both necessity and possibility. Normally, teachers are qualified in educational philosophy, instructional and content delivery systems, basic human development, and under normal circumstance concentrate on the central task of education transacted and embodied in the teaching/learning process. All programs of education should have a singleness of purpose to complement and not compete with existing entities and institutions. Education should not attempt to do the work of faith-based entities or become preoccupied with sectarian thinking. Neither should education encroach on the purview of parents unless they are obviously dysfunctional or criminally neglectful. In such cases, remedial and surrogate discipline and guidance may be required to make the teaching/learning process work effectively (Green 2009). However, teachers and educational leaders should not rigidly adhere to a set of beliefs and fail to demonstrate tolerance for other points of view. All tax supported educational activities should be non-sectarian, non-profit, and nondiscriminatory, but committed to the social and moral values of the community and society at large.

Teacher and Student Assessments

Without a level playing field, the system cannot adequately evaluate teacher competence and student achievements. New teachers who are given a class of misfits or delinquents may appear or feel inadequate and become discouraged with the profession while experienced teachers are advanced to the "easy learners" and self-starters. The quality and capacity of classroom instructions also impacts student learning. Because of many dysfunctional families, classroom teachers are often expected to compensate for parental and/or community failures. This is a burden that becomes a bridge too far for many teachers.

Classroom teachers should not be expected to do the work of parents or community authorities when their task is basic education. That task is to stimulate interest in the subject matter, arouse a spirit of inquiry, and get the student involved in the learning process. When teachers are forced to become disciplinarians or truant officers, to create an atmosphere conducive to learning, the teaching/learning process is hindered. Unacceptable classroom behavior distracts from classroom objectives and imposes deficiencies on the whole class. Teachers are weak substitutes for loving parents and the school classroom an atmosphere totally different from what exists in the local community.

There is no magic in the classroom that easily corrects home and community failures. In fact, parents and family are considered more important to academic achievement than are budgets, curriculum, teachers, textbooks or classroom equipment. However, where the family and previous instruction models have failed the student, educators must practice tough love and positive remedial education and seek to constructively and creatively solve the learning distractions of students. This must also include the general protection and welfare of the teaching staff and school property. All programs of education must encourage mutually beneficial relationships with parents, organizations, and communities which share the same basic moral values.

As a state or community sponsored program, the school system should provide directions for academic development and problem solving skills that are geared to the transitions demanded of students moving from a parent-based to a teacher-based learning model and then to a self-study process. This does not mean that parents are not involved in their children's education; it simply means that qualified teachers are guiding the process of a standardized educational program and seeking positive parental assistance. It means that parents must never neglect their children's education and must express concern and provide assistance regardless of the age-specific level of education involved. It also suggests that there will come a time when the student outgrows the need for classroom support and may become more dependent on guidance from the family before they can become an independent learner using all past learning to gain needed knowledge useful for a career or profession. However, students never outgrow their need for family or for academic guidance and encouragement. Without such direction and support that inspires confidence, the real world can become an intimidating place.

Regardless of classroom activities, learning is self-paced and should be flexible and structured to achieve optimum benefit from academic interface, independent study, parental assistance, faculty guidance and peer support. All students work from a personal knowledge base and experience to utilize classroom or subject content and enhance competence and performance. The teaching/learning interface should be structured to precipitate transformational change through aggressive learning and innovative instruction. The objective is to gain new knowledge which may be used to answer questions and used in present and future problem solving.

By analyzing the structure of the educational environment and society in general from the perspective of moral and ethical needs, a group of transformational learning leaders can make a difference in advancing beneficial changes in the objectives and practices of education. Such an educational program requires an evident balance between what educators believe and what students actually do. Thus, the curriculum and instruction must be related to the background of the student and appropriate to the community. It must be evenhanded, unprejudiced by present community problems, and adequately balanced with commitments to the past deposit of moral truth upon which ethical and moral behavior is based.

This commitment requires recognition of what constitutes past moral and ethical behavior, but in no way relieves supervisors and instructors of responsibility to understand present society and to seek solutions for current problems and learning difficulties. The system must clearly synthesize moral and ethical foundations of community into a philosophy of productive social change and service to society. The educational process should culminate in both an ethical and productive citizen who supports the common values of society. This is transformational education. Systematic teaching is a general term for a pedagogic-structured style of teaching which are preplanned to produce specific learning outcomes (Green 2007).

In the present age of technology and 24/7/365 exposure to global issues, to accomplish the transformational changes required to advance the teaching/learning process, the educational system must move beyond pedagogic methods to more advanced andragogic and synergetic learning designs. Andragogy is teaching students as mature learners regardless of age. It also includes the concept that education is not only vocational but general preparation for life and lifelong learning. Andragogy fosters the concept that education is a process that continues throughout life and is not limited to a classroom, age, or the presence of a teacher.

The concept of synergy is learning from one another and has impact on all aspects of peer interaction in education. Synergetic designs are a systematic approach to learning in which the members of small groups learn from one another through structured interactions; thus, the idea of synergy in learning. Challenge and stimulation are created through social situations where real and felt needs may be satisfied. All education must provide learning activities and materials from which knowledge or insights can be acquired and create designs—instructions for both individual and group action— that can stimulate learning. (Mouton 1984)

Conflict and Creativity

Transformational instruction must go beyond pedagogic methods to include the construct of **Synectics,** a term used in writing on creativity. Greek in origin, the word means the bringing together of separated and seemingly irrelevant ideas or information. It is a systematic attempt to search all aspects of a problem creatively. In reality it is the development of the creative capacity of a student. Brainstorming is one techniques used in this process. Synectics also involves using mechanisms that make the strange familiar and the familiar strange to extend the creative imagination. Traditional pedagogic methods should be used only in the early stages of education or when necessary to instruct, tutor or communicate new content and when a specialized competency is required to move forward.

The characters that make the Chinese word "conflict" include crisis and opportunity. The English word is less revealing but has some of the same concepts when one considers the synonyms; such as, contention, contest, struggle, etc. In other words conflict may lead one to become creative. Creativity and invention are required when the way forward is blocked or unseen. When an individual is able to handle conflict or two opposing concepts and somehow merge them into one new construct they are being creative. Some businesses are able to both sell a product and nurture customers, others combine competition with discipline and create opportunities that advance their market share, the founding fathers of the United States of America were able to combine freedom and accountability and establish an enduring and responsible nation. This idea has explosive meaning for education and the teaching/learning process.

The classroom model stands in opposition to the distance education mechanisms, and the pedagogic processes are counter-productive when over used with the more innovative models related to Andragogy and synergetic learning designs. When the emphasis on content overpowers process both teaching and learning are hindered. However, when an experienced teacher clearly understands the predisposition and maturity of learners, they can effectively combine pedagogy and the more interactive designs and greatly facilitate the learning process. When a teacher understands that the goal of teaching is to make the learner self-sufficient, the conflict is resolved and learning opportunities bust forth much as the morning sunrise does after a dark and stormy night.

The pioneer leaders of nations and the men and women of past generations invented, developed, manufactured, built, constructed, fought great wars, won significant victories, and achieved great things without the technological and scientific support available today. In a day when high school drop-outs can become National Network News Anchors, when men with "C" averages in education can be elected to the highest positions in the land, and when individuals leave college because they are bored with the process but create major corporations, it is time to rethink education and do everything possible to improve the teaching/learning process. Part of that improvement is to develop self-actualizing, self-paced, self-confident, and self-sufficient learners.

Assumptions about Serious Study

To learn from a written text, one must see the author of the text as a real person, a learning leader, and the text as an objective body of knowledge and utilize a methodical approach to comprehend the content. The information, facts, and data included in an objective text are distinct form the reader's interpretation. Consequently, the reader must be objective in viewing the written material. There is no absolute objectivity or pure induction; therefore, a systematic method is required to interpret written material. A student must view a written work from the author's perspective to arrive at a sound understanding. Subjectivity in analysis corrupts the intended meaning of the content. The author of a text must be considered a personal instructor with concern and interest in the reader. The author has many of the same qualities and concerns as does the classroom teacher (Green 2008).

Constructive change in education requires dynamic structures and mechanisms appropriate for the twenty-first century. Using transformational concepts, leaders can map a path to positive social change in the teaching/learning process and create a curriculum and instructional components that will open new thinking and learning patterns in the classroom and beyond.

CHAPTER ONE

Structure and Constructive Change

A basic structure to nurture relationships in education between the system oversight, the principal, the teachers, the students, and the parents is a four-step model referred to as form/storm/norm/perform. This path to constructive change is needed to adopt, deploy and ultimately bring forth positive change in the teaching/learning process. All involved in the educational arena must feel comfortable with the process and be open to new thinking and learning patterns for the vision of beneficial change to become a reality.

Changing the Atmosphere in the Classroom

The first step in the process of changing performance in the classroom is **to create an atmosphere conducive to learning.** This will require a drastic change in the status quo of the class. When the class is a little off balance, individual resistance is normally lessened. Three methods may achieve this change: (1) increase the driving forces that direct behavior away from the present situation. (2) decrease the restraining forces that negatively impact the change of the existing balance. (3) find a combination of the two methods and use constructive steps to produce change in the atmosphere. Create a vigorous discussion of the subject at hand, build trust and recognition for the need to change, and prepare the students for change.

Another step in changing behavior according to Kurt Lewin is **movement**. The teacher must move the class to a new level of balance. Three actions can assist in this process: (1) persuade students that their present attitude about the subject is not beneficial and encourage a fresh view of the whole subject; (2) produce new and relevant information on the subject at hand, and (3) portray well-respected authorities who value the subject. Once the attitude toward the subject has changed, assist the students with use of an application of the subject to real life situations. Place the driving and resisting forces in balance by demonstrating the value and usefulness of the subject. Build on the excitement and the spirit of inquiry to move the learning process forward. The classroom environment will change when the strength of the driving forces exceed the restraining forces (Robbins, 2003).

There are several steps in the change of attitude toward learning, but mainly in the classroom it is the teacher's responsibility.

1   Determine the problem and diagnose the capacity for change.
2   Develop action plans and establish strategies.
3   Maintain a positive attitude toward positive change.
4   Based on feedback and class participation, gradually step back into a more passive role.
5   Attitude change toward the classroom subjects is more easily maintained if the excitement of learning is shared in the home environment.
6   When learning becomes part of the family culture, it is more likely to be considered part of the normal process.
7   Provided the class and the home environment are excited about learning, the positive change is more likely to endure. (Lippitt, R., Watson, J. and Westley, B. 1958).

Intentionality and Reflection

An increased learning model is supported by intentionality

that moved from intention to consideration or reflection. When an individual student is not ready for greater involvement in classroom activities, some students may justify their attitude as being normal. However, when the teacher excites and directs the self-activity a student becomes aware of the value of the subject at hand. This precipitates positive change and the student begins to make preparation for learning. When students are ready they will need counseling, support, and assistance. Care must be taken to make learning an exciting part of the student's lifestyle.

Student Behavior

Students learn by doing, through dialogue and interaction, and observation. Classroom environmental factors, personal health, and the quality of instructions are vital to the teaching/learning process. To learn individuals must possess self-interest and have confidence in their capability to grow and develop. Also, they must see an incentive in learning and this enticement has to do with the future. Most students do not seek knowledge for knowledge sake but seek to know in order to perform effectively and become productive in a career or profession. The positive aspects of the learning environment must outweigh the negative expectations. If there are also immediate benefits, such as grades or awards, in addition to the future advantage and compensation, then the learning experience is more energized.

These long-term advantages create an atmosphere conducive to present learning. When an instructor is clear on the long-range advantage and takes a lesson from tennis that a player must score two successive points to win after the score is tied (deuce); the student will realize that energy and effort must be put into study and learning to ultimately achieve success in overcoming the difficulties of life. When this occurs, the student becomes an enthusiastic learner. The concept of self-interest determines a student's behavior because the expected outcomes are filtered through a desire to achieve not only the enthusiasm of the teacher but also the essential elements of the subject.

Learning Must Relate to the Future

Classroom teachers may present the essential elements of the study by (1) providing clear instructions, (2) modeling a scholarly demeanor, and (3) offering ways and means for growth and academic development. These processes include: (1) concentration, (2) preservation (2) reproduction, and (4) validation. **Concentration** involves attentiveness, awareness, and focus on paying attention to details. Students learn best when the material is presented in an attractive and compelling manner. **Preservation** includes maintenance and perpetuation of the process. **Reproduction** requires the student to duplicate the essential elements of the lesson and actively utilize the details of the subject. **Validation** includes justification of time and energy and providing support or corroboration for what was learned. Validation comes in a change of behavior and performance based on rewards and incentives. To enhance the learning process teachers must evoke trust, admiration, and respect from the students. The emphasis is on respect which means "to look at, pay attention to the person and the subject." There is no right or wrong way for a teacher to accomplish this task. All teachers are different and must continually review and consider how they approach a subject in the classroom.

A Contingency Model

Behavior or goal-directed activity in the teaching/learning process is dependent on factors and circumstances that are normally unknown. The structure of a classroom may be a relatively fixed process and the learning activities planned and arranged in advance, but the capacity for learning is determined by the combination of maturity, intellect, background and opportunity. Learning in the classroom is also dependent on the competence of the teacher and the motivation of the learner. Motivation is simply "motive" plus "action." When the learner's motives are understood, the teacher can present activities that enhance learning. What are the reasons capable of causing movement toward learning? How can the teacher attach the elements of the lesson to the life and present circumstance of the learner? What are the factors that cause movement in a positive direction? However, the personal maturity, the intellectual capacity of the learner, and the personal background and previous opportunities of the learner are factors in the learning process. The difficulty is that these are unknown factors and may not be directly measured; therefore, a process of surrogating on the part of the teacher must be employed to determine the knowledge base, the capacity, and the motivation of the learner. When these elements are known, the teacher is ready to initiate the teaching/learning cycle that begins with a form stage.

FORM	STORM	NORM	PERFORM
M1	M2	M3	M4

IMMATURE ───→ MATURE

Form/Storm/Norm/Perform   PLUS   Adjourn/Mourn/Reform Cycle

Figure 1. 1 –Original model compared with revised.

The **Form-Storm-Norm-Perform Model** was first proposed by Bruce Tuckman (1965) by synthesizing the literature in therapy groups, t-group studies and natural and laboratory groups. He noted that all of these groups tended to follow similar patterns during their development, and so followed on to identify the subsequent stages. Tuckman maintained that stages were necessary to assure growth, produce results and solve problems. This model became a basis for subsequent leadership designs. Tuckman later added a fifth phase, **Adjourning**, that involves completing the task or dissolving the group. Some call this stage, "**Mourning**" suggesting grief or sorrow, but the completion of a task or the advancement of an individual or class to another level should be a time of rejoicing; therefore, this writer chooses to call this stage, "**Morning**" suggesting a new beginning or a sunrise on a new opportunity. In education this stage is often called promotion, commencement or graduation.

Forming happens when people first come together. They are initially polite and the conversation is mostly exploratory, finding out about one another and the work that is to be done. This is the first stage of group or class building when the members are uninformed of the objectives and goals requiring a facilitator to be instructive. Members of the group or class begin as individuals and are focused on themselves. This process can take a few days or stretch over a much longer period. The role of the facilitator or teacher is not to jump straight to perform but to facilitate this social process and speed the group through the four stages.

Facilitating the Forming stage is best done by informing the group/class of the specific agenda. The members are dependent and must be instructed as to the value and purpose of the subject at hand. The work to be done should be communicated in a way that facilitates an understanding of what is to be achieved without overwhelming with detail. This is not the time for fellowship or the building of friendship among the group. Each member of the group/class must be seen as an individual with personal worth and value. One does not teach a class, a subject, or a text; neither can a group be instructed. The use of a "splatter-shot" approach that attempts to cover the whole group will not produce positive outcomes. Only individuals may be taught. Only individuals learn. Consequently, all instructors must know and understand each individual they wish to guide in the learning process.

Storming is a stage of competition where group/class members open up to each other and challenge other member's view of the subject or task. As individual members of a class get involved in learning they may agree or disagree with others on the subject at hand. Conflict or disagreements should be viewed a kind of brain-storming. This is a period when individuals are counter dependent meaning what they are learning is based on their personal knowledge base. Such aggressive interaction should be seen as a healthy discussion and a major asset to the learning process. This is where students learn from one another and begin to trust the views of others.

Normally there will be one or two students who stand out intellectually and will make a bid to control the discussion. When this occurs, the storm stage is in full bloom. The maturity level of members determine if or when the group moves out of this phase of development. This stage can be contentious and unpleasant and without tolerance and patience the group/class will fail or at best lower the motivation level to learn. Instructors must remain directive and interact with both individuals and the group until the group maturity level is sufficient to move to the next stage. This happens when a majority of the group/class has understood the lesson and those who do not comprehend are identified and assisted. This requires both high relationship and high task.

The instructor should resolve differences that could cause problems with group cohesion. Storming may also be reduced by clarifying objectives, goals and individual roles. When people are clear on these, they become more focused and can begin the process of moving forward to the process of individual excitement in learning various aspects of the subject. This is movement toward the norm of the teaching/ learning process.

Norming is a stage where individual learning becomes natural behavior and members of the group agree on behavior guideline and begin to trust each other and value learning opportunities. As students learn the part they play in the social and learning context, they are able to function independently and learn the essential elements of the subject at hand. Learning objectives are clarified and details of the future value of the subject matter are worked out. Feeling more a part of the class, individuals begin to cooperate. Group rules develop and are refined as individuals work together in the learning process. Individuals begin to feel an *espirt de corps* and a clear sense of identity emerges.   Motivation for the task at hand increases. To prevent the group/class from becoming stifled by groupthink, instructors need to participate more in the function of the group/class. As learning goals are achieved, some members may feel they have learned enough and may develop a resistance to moving forward.

During norm stage, the instructor should focus less on task and more on relationships and create an atmosphere for learning and exchange. Teaching objectives and learning goals will progress as individuals feel comfortable in their roles and in working with others. Group norms and behaviors may be deliberately developed as the individuals prepare for more advanced achievement and the group begins to sense definite progress toward personal performance.

Performing is a stage of achievement for both individual members and the group/class and the learning activities are accomplished without conflict or the need for supervision. A steady-state system is achieved when the class reaches a maximum level of performance. A good group/class will develop a sense of family and begin to show concern for individuals being left behind in the learning process. When individuals begin to assist others in understanding and accomplishing the learning activities, the perform stage is operational. As students develop the knowledge that they can learn from one another a level of maturity is developed and learning becomes exciting and useful. The group/class becomes interdependent and supervision is always participative and decision making is delegated to the members.   Changing circumstances can cause a team to revert to storming as new members are added to the group, the teacher drastically changes his/her attitude and behavior, or the task or subject changes. The maturity of individuals speaks to the overall maturity of the group and determines the level of participation in the learning process.

TPR Model – Further developments

White and Fairhurst examined Tuckman's stages and simplified the sequence. Their model was to group **(Forming-Storming-Norming)** into one stage as a **Transforming** phase. White and Fairhust saw their **Transforming** phase as equal to the initial **Performance** level. Their initial phase was followed by a **Performing** stage that produced a new performance level they called the **Reforming** phase. This process was called the White-Fairhurst TPR Model. This model was further developed in 2008 by White when he demonstrated the linkage between Tuckman's work and that of Colin Carnall's Comfort Zone Theory. The Transforming-Performing-Reforming (TPR) Model would then be: **(Forming/Storming/Norming)** plus **(Performing)**, plus **(Reforming).** An achieving individual or group may go beyond to a **Transforming** stage. Transformational leadership produces change in performance through a sense of synergy. This working together (synergy) is considered an effective level of performance. At times there may be a **Reforming** stage. These additions create a more comprehensive model as compared with the original. (Tuckman, 1965; White, 2008)

Additional stages

The **Adjourn** stage could be called the **disbanding** phase of group activity or in education: promotion, graduation, or commencement. Toward the end of the normal time a group functions, members become concerned about the end game: disbanding or reforming the group. Perhaps this is where the concept of "class reunion" was developed. A feeling of separation anxiety develops and a sense of crisis intrudes on the group. This sense of crisis brings about both difficult choices and opportunities to move forward. The old gang may wish to stay together and, when advisors attempt to guide them according to their achievements and goals, they may meet with hostility. External facilitators can be confused by the refusal to change or consider a future different than the present. Just as ceremony and customary procedures assisted with initiating the process of education and giving of achievement recognition along the way, the same practices may assist the group/class to cope with the changes at the end. This is why education instituted awards, honors, certificates, diplomas, and degrees. Guidance counseling, career advice, and qualifying exams assist in preparing students for the next logical step.

A **deform** phase sometimes happens during the adjourment stage when the facilitator assumes a low relationship and low task posture too soon. It may also happen when new people join the group or key people leave the group and the established social order is upset. After an adjournment or deforming process, the group may **reform** and go quickly through the form-storm-norm-perform cycle to cope with the loss of key people or to absorb the new members. This process may cause a **mourning** which is the grieving for the loss of special relationships. This writer prefers to drop the "u" and call this stage "morning" because it is a new beginning and a fresh start for everyone concerned. There are experienced individuals prepared and ready for a new task just waiting for opportunity to knock gently on their front door or they are ready to rush out into the real world of work and achievement. Following the end-game for each group/class or cohort, the transformational leader welcomes a new group of individuals to the teaching/learning process. This opportunity introduces new obligations for the teacher to introduce, instruct, inspire, and apply the essential elements of a subject to the life and future of the learner. This is the beginning of transformational leadership in education.

FORM	STORM	NORM	PERFORM
Why we are here	Bid for power	Constructive	Esprit de Corps
	COUNTER		
DEPENDENT	DEPENDENT	INDEPENDENT	INTERDEPENDENT
Mutual acceptance	Decision making	Motivation	Cohesive
STAGE ONE	STAGE TWO	STAGE THREE	STAGE FOUR

IMMATURE ───────────────────────────────────▶ MATURE

Figure 1.2 – Stages of the Teaching/Learning Cycle

Repeating the Teaching/Learning Cycle

At the close of each term or even a class session, the teacher must develop a positive attitude toward a new group/class. Following the end-game for each cohort, the transformational leader welcomes a new group of individuals to the teaching/ learning process. A new group/class goes through an awareness phase similar to the **Form** stage during orientation, because the new group has an immaturity because of the change of environment, subject, or location. This new or reformed group will go through the same process as other newly formed groups. The leader's behavior is High Task/ Low Relationship. There will be a **Storm** or conflict phase for the new group. The leader's behavior is High Task/High Relationship. The key is to work through the storming stage by developing methods for handling conflict: dialogue and consensus decision-making are the strongest methodologies.

This period of resistance is followed by cooperation and cohesion known as the **Norm** phase. The leader's behavior is High Relationship/Low Task. As interdependence develops, a period of productivity is enjoyed normally seen as the **Perform** stage. The leader's behavior is Low Task/Low Relationship. It should be remembered that the leader's behavior should be determined by the maturity of the group during each phase of development.

CHAPTER TWO

Transformational Leadership and Education

Transformational Leadership

Transformational leadership in education is constructive change that transforms the teaching/learning process using both the maturity of the student and the expertise of the teacher. The goal is a wiser use of the energy of the teacher and the learner by providing more effective processes and more appropriate content. The course of action includes guiding, directing and influencing a student, a group of students, teachers, and administrators in the direction of positive development and constructive change in the learning process.

The transformational aspects of education are guided by the strengths of both teacher and learner. It is a strengths-based approach to education that acknowledges the background and intellectual experience of the administrative staff, the teacher, and the learner. The curriculum is designed as a vehicle to move the learner in a positive direction based on prior knowledge and maturity. Instructors have flexibility within the core curriculum based on learner maturity to identify and utilize strengths and interest of learners and facilitate intellectual growth based on these areas within the broad construct of a program of study.

Educational direction and leadership are determined by the maturity of the class or the individuals involved and the expertise of the person in charge whether in administration or the classroom. The process requires an understanding of the sympathetic factors working automatically within the class or individuals that create a synergy or a working together. Much as the autonomic nervous system of the human body, certain factors are at work in every group, class, and within each individual. This function is normally below the conscious level. If educational leaders, whether they be superintendent, principal, teacher or aide, are not aware of this process their ability to influence others to follow their direction voluntarily is limited.

An automatic process below the conscious level appears to be working to either inhibit or excite certain behavior and mental functions. The total background and experience unconsciously controls some of the thinking and action of individuals. Those functioning in leadership roles should be aware of this process. Also there are the cybernetic or triggered aspects of interactive behavior that deal with a feedback system in the process of the teaching/learning exchange. An understanding of these deeper constructs of behavior and feedback are essential to transformational education. This may produce major changes in performance through a more advanced working together that affects all concerned than simple transactional instruction which is interactivity between two or more individuals.

Transformational leadership in education produces significant constructive change in teacher and student behavior and is more effective in producing learning outcomes. The elements of the transformational construct are found in the combined words of Gardner, Einstein, and Emerson. John W. Gardner once said "A prime function of a leader is to keep hope alive." And Einstein claimed that setting an example was the "only means" of influencing others. Emerson added the building block of "enthusiasm" as an essential construct in achievement. Although many others have written about leadership, the combination of the elements of hope, example, and enthusiasm seem to summarize the background of transformational leadership that creates the ability to influence others to follow voluntarily toward stated goals in education. To be influenced toward productivity, students must be exposed to a good example, see genuine enthusiasm in the instructor, and be convinced of a hopeful future.

The transformational construct has been a major aspect and in some cases the primary influence in recent organizational models. Since drastic and dramatic changes are needed in most educational systems, the transformational paradigm is appropriate in education. The origin of transformational leadership has been traced to James McGregor Burns in his discussion of capacity in leaders to motivate staff to function with energy and enthusiasm related to organizational objectives (Burns, 1978). A servant approach to leadership is added to make the leader's priority to serve others first and the organization second.

Transformational leadership was designed to develop the capability to innovate in an organization and to build capacity to revise purpose or mission statements in an effort to support positive change in the teaching/learning environment. The focus is on a shared vision and constructive change. Transformational leadership seeks to build commitment to objectives and to empower others regardless of their level in the organization to work toward reaching institutional, group, and individual objectives.

Since transformational leadership and servant leadership are similar, the big question is how do they differ? The difference seems to be based on the predisposition of the leaders. Transformational leaders are engaged in the support of organizational objectives while servant leaders demonstrate more concern for the individuals involved. It is at this point that the function of transformational leadership in education differs from the behavior of other organizational leaders. In education everyone in leadership must maintain a positive attitude toward students and their predisposition should demonstrate a genuine concern for the teaching/learning process and the learning outcomes. Business and industry may be able to selective eliminate non-productive workers, but the educational community has no such authority. Teachers who cannot teach and students who do not learn remain in the system.

This is where transformational leadership can influence education: weak teachers must be improved and all students given an opportunity to advance from where they are to where they need to be. When individuals feel a "call" to the teaching profession as a lifelong journey, their abilities and techniques can be enhanced. Those who see teaching as a temporary "job" create most of the difficulties in the classroom. When students factor in the future and clearly see the value and impact of the present lesson on their personal future, most can be guided toward improvement in study habits and learning skills.

Leaders in education place great stock in parental involvement as a predictor of academic achievement. In areas where parents or guardians are not active in the educational transaction, transformational leadership can be effective in achieving parental participation. If one adds to the mix that educational leadership at all levels must have a care and concern for the students, where parental involvement is an objective of the system, transformational leadership can bring meaningful change to education. Since the world has become complicated and global changes affect every corner of the earth, transformational leaders with a servant heart can be beneficial in the current educational environment.

Two constructs stand out in the literature of leadership: transactional or leadership based on tangible rewards and leaders using transformational strategies to engage followers with basic needs and achievement outcomes. Some scholars affirm that good leaders demonstrate characteristics of both of these constructs (Judge and Piccolo, 2004).

A Note of Warning

Transformational leadership has the potential for abuse based on the morality of the leader. This may be true of all leadership functions; that is, the ability to influence others to follow them regardless of the direction they travel. However, provided leaders avoid dictatorial or oppressive behavior, the ability to make constructive change associated with transformational leadership far outweighs any risk of abuse. "To bring about change, authentic transformational leadership fosters the modal values of honesty, loyalty, and fairness, as well as the end values of justice, equality, and human rights" (Griffin,2003). There is also a concern that teachers could be distracted from the teaching/learning process by becoming overly involved working on the objectives initiated by the administration.

There is a dichotomy in ethics: one view relates ultimate causes in nature or actions in relation to their utility and the other relates to philosophical theories that state that the moral content of an action is not wholly dependent on its consequences. An ethical teacher who cares about the student can normally proportion their time between institutional objectives and the goals of the teaching/learning process. The force that placed an individual in the teaching profession is primarily related to a concern for the student and this takes precedent over concern for the institution. Some scholars affirm that ethical decision-making is best found using both approaches illustrated by the dichotomy (Israel and Hay, 2006).

Transformational leadership seeks to find new ways of implementing change while at the same time building the morale of workers and students. Other leadership theories have operated for several decades; such as, traits-based leadership, behavior-based, and contingency theories related to life-cycle dynamics. Although these theories worked in ordinary situations, they did not provide the energetic leadership necessary to produce constructive change or redefine the vision or mission of an organization, or produce an encouragement stimulus and an incentive to follow the guidance of a moral leader; therefore, it is assumed that transformational leadership has a moral foundation.

The definition of transformational leadership in the existing literature include constructs; such as, influence, personal motivation, mental stimulation, needs assessment, corporate visions, and participative decision-making. Transformational leadership fosters capacity to enable workers to be more productive and a general awareness of the objectives of the organization. Productivity and awareness are done by knowing where each person stands in relation to Maslow's hierarchy of needs. This knowing includes the desire to learn, make a difference, and leave a legacy.

Beyond Maslow's formally ranked group of five, higher levels of needs exist. These include needs for understanding, aesthetic appreciation, and purely spiritual needs. A key aspect of Maslow's model is the hierarchical nature. The lower the needs in the hierarchy, the more fundamental they are and the more a person will tend to abandon the higher needs in order to sufficiently meet the lower needs. If for example, one is hungry or ill or does not feel safe or loved or suffers from low self-esteem, that individual cannot participate in the learning process or achieve individual potential. This means that a transformational learning environment must take into account the levels of need below self-actualization to insure an effective teaching/learning process. Maslow later added three more needs by splitting two of the original five needs.

Between esteem and self-actualization three additional needs were identified:

5. Self-actualization needs are to realize personal growth and fulfillment.

---

*   Need to know and understand which includes the acquisition of knowledge and intellectual and scholarly growth.
*   The need for aesthetic beauty which is part of the emotional and affective domain.
*   Self-actualization was divided into realizing one's own potential and transcendence, which reaches for quality and assists others to achieve.

Needs 1-4 must be met for learning to occur.

4. Esteem includes achievement, status, responsibility, reputation.
3. Belonging includes family, relationships, affection
2. Safety includes protection, security, and stability.
1. Physiological includes basic life needs: food, shelter, warmth, sleep, and love.

Confidence in a leader is required for people to accept institutional constituency or change. This produces the clear meaning of leadership as the ability to influence others to follow one voluntarily toward stated goals. This means that a transformational leader can influence the entire constituency of an organization by planning for the future and taking advantage of each opportunity to advance toward a positive future. When this occurs, problem solving is on the back burner and is normally handled as a routine matter necessary to move forward. This process enables the constituency to develop a positive mindset that is predictive of productivity and progress.

A transformational leader has the vision for positive social change and a voice to articulate an attractive and alternative future. With both vision and voice, such leaders are able to influence innovative thinking and positive action toward constructive change. Such leaders provide careful consideration of individual problems and are able to utilize the strengths of individuals to build both personal confidence and corporate productivity. Strengths are used to compensate for weaknesses. When both weaknesses and strengths are determined, normally one can use existing strengths to compensate for apparent weaknesses. Opportunities are utilized to minimize problems. These various constructs have an additive effect on the constituency of an organization and moves individuals beyond problems to a positive future.

Normally, a transformational leader has a value driven sense of purpose with high expectations and a persistent and self-knowing personality.   They maintain a present desire and enthusiasm to learn. These leaders are enthusiastic, able to inspire others and they listen to all viewpoints and demonstrate a spirit of cooperation.   They are usually courageous risk-takers and have a sense of what is best for the common good. Complexity and uncertainty do not hinder the perception of themselves as a change agent.

A transformational leader can precipitate significant change in the constituency of an organization. Such leaders change the institutional culture, improve mission statements, and structure a strategy for constructive change. This is normally done by leaders making a strong case for change by sharing a common vision and through collaboration building the self-confidence of individuals.   They act optimistically by sharing both their vision and their values by asking relevant questions. What can be done new? What can be done differently? What can be done better? Transformational leaders are able to deal constructively with the resistance to change by pointing to a progressive future with new and advanced opportunities for all involved.

Transformational characteristics have been around for centuries. World history has recorded significant change related to individual leaders in many generations, including Genghis Khan, George Washington, Abraham Lincoln, John Milton Gregory, John Dewey, Lee Iacocca, and more recently Barack Obama. The distinctive nature of transformational leadership is not impeded by local or institutional culture but does depend somewhat on cultural values. Without certain values an organization may not be able to see the advantages of change and progress. Within the educational environment, it is the teachers who are more likely to collaborate and have positive attitudes toward school improvement and new forms of instructional behavior as a result of transformational leadership.

Three positive examples of transformational leadership in education, the military and government are Dr. Ruth Simmons, General Colin Powell, and Dr. Condoleezza Rice. These and many others have used transformational leadership to advance performance beyond expectations and produce significant changes in individuals and organizations. Negative examples also exist, but patterns of socially unacceptable behavior are not the purview of this book.

Dr, Simmons was born in Grapeland, Texas, the last of 12 children and became the first African-American to be appointed President of an "Ivy League" university in the USA. Before arriving at Brown University, she served as a Dean at Princeton, Provost at Spellman College and President of Smith College where she started the first American engineering program at a women's university. Simmons was a transformational leader and attributed her achievements to a kindergarten teacher, who told her she could do anything she set her heart to achieve.

General Powell, born in Harlem, New York to immigrant Jamaican parents, overcame racism to become a four-star General in the United States Army, Chairman of the US Joint Chiefs of Staff and the first African-American United States Secretary of State, a position he filled with the qualities and influence of a transformational leader.

Dr. Rice was born into a minority family in Alabama and became a professor, diplomat, author, and national security expert. She was the first woman of African descent to serve as United States Secretary of State. Before her government service, Dr. Rice was a professor of political science at Stanford University where she also served as Provost for six years. As United States Secretary of State, Dr. Rice pioneered a policy of Transformational Diplomacy, with a focus on democracy in the Middle East and has returned to Stanford as a professor and a Senior Fellow on Public Policy at the Hoover Institution.

There is an emerging trend in the literature suggesting a blend of the 3T's: transactional, transformational, and transcendental leadership (Sanders, Hopkins and Geroy 2003). They suggested a model with three dimensions: spirituality, consciousness, with moral character and faith. It is understood that most current models of leadership are based on external expressions of leadership, but the missing component could be the leader's internal spiritual qualities. The addition of the transcendental is to bring an area of philosophy that is independent of human experience, but within the range of knowledge. This construct is included in Sympathetic Leadership Cybernetics (Green, 2007).

The need for life applications for that which is learned is related to the learning process. Understanding how guidance, maturity and the nature of teaching influences learning is discussed together with the impact of factors that operate automatically in the mind and life of the learner and how these changes impact the teacher's behavior. Both the formal and the informal aspects of the teaching/learning process are addressed with an emphasis on the affective domain. Certain underlining assumptions about education are presented and Miller's Living Systems Theory (LST) is applied to the teaching/learning process. In summary this work presents a basic philosophy of education and the structure of constructive change in the teaching/learning process. Maturity is determined by considering task and relationship factors.

TASK	"What's the task?" "Why am I here?" "Why are you here?" "I've got other things to do!"	Emotional response to task "I don't like it." "I like it." "Why do we do it this way?"	Roles defined Method of sharing resources worked out Work load divided and Coordination of work	Solutions to problems Highly efficient productive Job done well with minimum effort
RELATION-SHIP	Testing, probing one another and leader Lessening the mistrust	Group checks leader's credibility if it doesn't like the task Polarization of group Cliques develop in groups Learning to trust others	Polarities and cliques dissolve Group begins to operate as a group Cliques and individuals begin to listen Begin to block out non-group members	Group energy focused on task Relationship taken care of automatically Relationship between members is supportive of each other and the task
BEHAVIOR OF GROUP	Mutual acceptance DEPENDENT	Decision making COUNTER DEPENDENT	Constructive INDEPENDENT	Cohesiveness/ Control INTER-DEPENDENT
STAGES	FORM Why we're here	STORM Bid for power	NORM Motivation	PERFORM Esprit de corps

IMMATURE..MATURE

Figure 2.1—Teacher and class maturity

Since changes take place during the life cycle of the group, leadership hinges so completely on the interaction of task and relationship, a clear understanding of these two terms is essential:

Task Behavior – the extent to which a leader is likely to organize and define the roles of the members of a group (students); to explain what activities they are to do and when, where, and how tasks are to be accomplished, characterized by endeavoring to establish well-defined patterns of organization, channels of communication, and ways of getting tasks accomplished.

Relationship Behavior – the extent to which a leader is likely to maintain personal relationships between himself/herself and the members of his group (followers) by opening up channels of communications, delegating responsibility, giving subordinates an opportunity to use their potential; characterized by socio-emotional support, friendship, and mutual trust.

Leadership based on the contingency constructs of Living Systems Theory (LST) postulates that the teacher's behavior should move systematically through four stages. Form I, high task – low relationship; Storm II, high task – high relationship; Norm III, low task – high relationship; and Perform IV, low task – low relationship, which coincide with the movement of the class through the four developmental stages previously described. Individual students will also move through these phases. (See Chapter Three for more discussion of LST.)

The behavior of the teacher/leader then becomes, expressed in the simplest terms, akin to choosing a meal in a Chinese restaurant: complementary dishes from Column A and Column B (Task and Relationship). Depending on the observed and anticipated behavior of the group, the four basic leadership behaviors can be used effectively in order to get the best possible output regardless of the stage of group formation. Appropriate behavior is described in terms of task and relationship for each stage of maturity. The leader models the stage behavior appropriate for the maturity level of the class.

1. Model high commitment to task. 2. Set goals. 3. State expectations 4. Encourage disclosure of resources in relation to task. 5. Demand commitment and accountability.	1. Allow emotional response to the task to take place. 2. Identify the coalitions/polarizations. 3. Explain that consequences are unacceptable 4. Respond to credibility check honestly – don't punish. 5. Negotiate an understanding or seek outside source to assist in moving block. 6. Maintain congruence and high concern for all members.	1. Encourage role selected by individuals. 2. Encourage group consensus. 3. Roles may be different for short term focus than long, also for different environment. 4. Take advantage of opportunities.	1. Allow group to perform. 2. Encourage those things which prevent boredom. 3. Focus on environmental conditions which can be changed to produce more challenge. 4. Plan for the future.
High Task – Low Relationship	High Task – High Relationship	Low Task – High Relationship	Low Task – Low Relationship
MATURITY 1	MATURITY 2	MATURITY 3	MATURITY 4
FORM	STORM	NORM	PERFORM

IMMATURE   MATURE

Figure 2.2– Changes in teacher behavior based on class maturity

Education Has Come Full Circle

Education has come full circle since John Milton Gregory (1822-1998) observed that **the best classroom was nothing more than a good teacher on one end of a log and a pupil on the other.** In addition to his seven laws of teaching, Gregory had other timeless insights with universal application. Not realizing the impact of the future technology on education, Gregory's statement about the log with a teacher on one end and the pupil on the other has direct application to the present D.I.A.L. System (Directed Internet Assisted Learning used by Oxford Graduate School in Tennessee and OASIS University in Trinidad as well as other technically advanced institutions. In D.I.A.L. a student uploads assignments to an Internet site and the professor logs into the sight and evaluates and grades the assignments. This interactive process is literally Gregory's log coming full circle.

CHAPTER THREE

Living Systems and Education

A Systems View of Teaching and Learning

A systems view of education is presented based directly on James Grier Miller's (1979) synthesis of Living Systems Theory (LST).   All concepts may not be articulated with the same attention to detail and example, but a core of basic concepts are identified. This introduction may spark the interest of educators for continuing study. Such a study could accelerate an understanding of the domain that science brings to the teaching/learning process. The language of systems analysis and education is introduced in an integrated fashion. This pedagogical method provides a framework for associating these concepts with those presently existing in education.

This introduction to some basic concepts of systems thinking shows the constructs of a system to be sufficiently general to be used to discuss various aspects of the teaching/ learning process in an integrated and coherent fashion. This is important to educators because it aids in sifting through numerous seemingly conflicting "facts" and methodologies used to study the various levels of relationship and interaction. It is assumed that LST is a useful general theory to guide the sorts of integrated, practical exploration done in the classroom.

A Functioning Classroom Environment

Miller's general LST theory postulated how living systems function, maintain themselves, develop, and change. By definition, living systems are open, self-organizing systems that have the special characteristics of existence and interact with their environment. This takes place by means of information and material-energy exchanges. This appears to be similar to a functioning classroom environment and the teaching/learning process.

Living systems can be as simple as a single cell or as complex as a supranational organization (such as the European Economic Union). Regardless of their complexity, they each depend upon the same essential twenty subsystems (or processes) in order to survive and to continue the propagation of their species or types beyond a single generation. Some of these processes deal with material and energy for the metabolic processes of the system. Other subsystems process information for the coordination, guidance and control of the system. Some subsystems and their processes are concerned with both matter/energy and information. A systems approach in education is the conscious use of systems analysis and systems design techniques in an effort to identify and solve complex problems in instructional or learning mechanisms. The components of the approach include the establishment of a systems boundary, the identification of all actual or possible inputs and outputs to the system and examination of their interacting and interrelated elements.

Some see education as all content, but the essence of life is process. The same is true of learning; learning is a process. If the processing of material-energy and information ends, life also ends. The defining characteristic of life is the ability to maintain, for a significant period, a steady state in which the entropy (or disorder) within the system is significantly lower than its non-living surroundings.

Living systems can maintain their energetic state because they are open, self-organizing systems that can take in from the environment the inputs of information and material-energy as needed. In general, living systems process more information than non-living systems, with the possible exception of computers which have greater information processing capabilities. Another fundamental difference between living and non-living systems is that all living systems have, as essential components, DNA, RNA, protein and some other complex organic molecules that give biological systems their unique properties. These molecules are not synthesized in nature outside of cells.

Definition of Systems

The universe of existence is obviously composed of many different elements. For example, every snowflake has a unique pattern and each human being has fingerprints and genetic codes different from those of any other person. In fact, science is hard pressed to find two identical specimens of anything. To establish a teaching style based solely on differentiation would be to consign the process of instruction to an infinite number of approaches and would be useless. Consequently, education while interested in differentiation moves the teaching/learning process forward by establishing commonalties among students.   These commonalties become the basis for structuring principles and standards of presenting content and concepts to students. Since learning proceeds from the known to the unknown, the identification of commonalties among students makes it possible for a teacher to reduce the teaching/learning overload to a manageable and useful level.

The systems view of existence is a set of definitions, concepts, and terminology of such a general nature that it is possible to use it to discuss, analyze, and synthesize specific aspects of education. Consequently, this view makes it possible to integrate and categorize what we have learned about teaching and learning from various experiences in other disciplines.

The concept of a system is obviously fundamental. The term system refers to any set of related and interacting elements. This is an extremely broad definition and, at the same time, sufficiently precise to be useful in education. The elements of a system can be anything. The important notion is that relationships among elements can be identified. The relationships of some simple systems may be mathematically identified, while the ability to relate, identify, and reduce to comprehensible complexity the relationships of highly complex living systems is still beyond the ability of most mathematicians.

While a basic definition of Living Systems could be expanded, it is sufficient for the context of education to understand the two basic qualities to which a system owes its existence, i.e., that of relationship and interacting elements. Relationship is a necessary but not sufficient quality for the teaching/learning process to work. For the process to function adequately, the elements must also be interdependent. Consequently, in the relationship between teacher and learner there is more than rapport, communication, and content. In addition to relationship, there are interdependent elements; that is, the actions of one must influence the actions of the other. The teaching/learning process is a two-way street. The teacher communicates both interest in the subject and content, but the student must provide feedback through a demonstrated interest, a spirit of inquiry, and evidence of participation through discussion, written reviews, homework, and evaluations.

Three Major Types of Systems

All systems are divided into three classes: concrete (complex) systems, abstracted (selected) systems, and conceptual (words, symbols, numbers) systems.

 A *concrete* system is a complex nonrandom accumulation of matter, energy, and information in a physical space-time, and organized into interacting, interrelated subsystems or components. Examples of concrete systems in education are teacher, curriculum, student, building and classroom equipment, classroom environment, and the human body. A concrete system is sophisticated and impossible to fully or completely comprehend. Who fully understands the dynamics of the interacting elements of teaching/learning process? All knowledge is limited and fragmented and must be associated with other data to be useful. Only selected parts of a *concrete* system based on prior knowledge may be studied.

An *abstracted* system is a limited set of relationships abstracted or selected by an observer in a particular environment. Abstracted (selected) systems are studied by *conceptual* systems. Examples of abstracted systems in education are a teacher's knowledge of a subject, a student's intellectual capacity, the operational elements of a curriculum, a lesson plan, class notes, or a student's reading comprehension or study capacity. Such abstracted (selected) systems are divided into two sub-types: a) those that may be directly measured, and b) those that must be assessed or evaluated through surrogated means. For example, answers to a quiz of 100 questions may be judged correct or incorrect and counted for a grade, but it does not measure the student's knowledge on the subject. It is a snap shot of what the student recalls about particular questions. This can be illustrated by a young boy explaining a poor test grade, "Daddy, the teacher didn't ask me the things I knew about the subject, she only asked me things I didn't know." Since all knowledge is limited, the difficulty in written exams is to ask the proper or appropriate questions that deal with the essential elements of the subject at hand and to use the quiz as a written review or learning tool. In fact, the exams are really an evaluation of the complete teaching/learning process that includes the competency of both teacher and learner. If no learning took place, then no teaching occurred. In fact it would be fair to grade the teacher on the student's ability to answer essential questions.

A *conceptual* system is a set of words, symbols, or numbers, used to explain an abstracted or selected system. Since the meaning of words is in people; that is, individuals have their own personal dictionary they use to understand classroom language. Does everyone understand all the symbols used in written material or math? What about > greater than or < less than? Do all students understand the &, @, #,. i.e., etc.? What about Roman Numerals or the points and sub-points of an outline (I. II., A. B., 1., 2. ,3., a), b)., 1)., 2),, etc.? Do all students understand the subordination or the value of these letters and numbers? A lack of understanding of words, symbols, or numbers complicates communication and learning.

Measured, *abstracted* systems are selected by a teacher by comparing elements of a concrete system with some standard or unit of a scale contained in the concrete system. Examples include the speed of an automobile moving 30 mph, the number of students reading in a library, and the observed number of students attending a sports event. In the first example, a speedometer compares the distance over which the automobile is moving with the units of the mile scale and, simultaneously, compares the distance measured to units of the hour time scale. By metering distance, clocking time, and connecting the two results according to understood mathematical operations, this equipment is able to supply the derived measurement of speed on demand.

Surrogated, *abstracted* systems are selected by a teacher who compares elements of a *conceptual* system with those of a *concrete* system, for instance, honesty, fear, an essay, a mathematical equation, purchasing power of lunch money, or a number-based grade on an exam are not actual measurements. Because there is no direct observer comparison between *concrete* elements (a numerical scale) and the actual grade, there is no assurance that the surrogated measurements are drawn from a given *concrete* system. The strength of surrogated abstractions rest with the ingenuity of the argument constructed to relate the *concrete* system elements to the *conceptual* system elements. This is why the normal grading system based on an arbitrary number does not directly measure either the intellectual capacity or the full knowledge of the student on a given subject. What is needed is a realistic assessment of the essential elements of a subject.

The Structure of Living Systems

A fundamental concept in general systems theory is the notion of emergence and interaction. A system is defined as a set of interacting interrelated elements. The properties (or behavior) of a system as a whole emerge out of the interaction of the components comprising the system. In the conceptual system developed by Miller, living systems form eight (8) levels of organization and complexity, ranging, as indicated earlier, from the simple cell to the supranational organizations. The best known single cell animal is the amoeba. This can be contrasted with the United Nations or the International Monetary Fund.

The eight levels of living systems are **cells** a basic building block of life; **organs** the principle components are cells organized in simple, multi-cellular systems; **organisms** there are three kinds of organisms: fungi, plants and animals. Each has distinctive cells, tissues and body plans and carries out life processes differently; **groups** contain two or more organisms and their relationships; **organizations** involve one of more groups with their own control systems for doing work; **communities** include both individual persons and groups, as well as groups which are formed and are responsible for governing or providing services to them; **societies** are loose associations of communities, with systematic relationships between and among them; **supranational** systems are organizations of societies with a supraordinate system of influence and control.

1.	Cells- made of atoms, molecules, and organelles
2.	Organs -made of cells

3.	**Organisms -composed of organs. (Individual student)**
4.	**Groups - made of organisms. (class or learning cohort)**
5.	**Organizations - have groups as components (school, grades,class cohorts)**
6.	**Communities - have organizations as components (school system)**

7.	Societies - have organizations and communities as parts
8.	Supranational systems - complexes of societies

Figure 3.1 - Living systems exist in a hierarchy of complexity

Living systems exist in a hierarchy of complexity from the cell to the supranational system.   Unless one is teaching biology, chemistry, or medicine, levels 1 and 2 are not of interest. Most teachers would be interested in levels numbers 3-6. Unless one is teaching graduate students, levels 7 and 8 are not of interest. Most teachers are concerned with individual students at the "organism" level, class and learning cohorts at the "group" level, a school and classes at the "organization" level, and perhaps some in education have interest in a particular school system at the "community" level. The complexity of the supranational system is beyond the scope of all studies below the research doctorate.

Individuals, Groups, and Classes (Organizations)

Educational leadership is concerned with the levels of organisms (individuals), groups, and classes (organizations) as they deal with the culture of the learning environment. As new people come into the system or an existing classroom, there is a time-lag in adjusting to the culture. Teachers and educational leaders must be sensitive to this phenomenon. One may appropriately translate the early education timeframe of months into years in an application to education of the individual.

A child has a period of socialization during the first 6 months of life in which the infant develops a relationship with authority. During the next 6 months the child develops a sense of expectation from the environment. At about one year the child begins to develop autonomy: walking, talking, and thinking about the environment. This process continues in annual growth and may be recognized in years.

As a child enters school at an early age it takes about 6 months to learn the rules and develop relationships with authority. This is called socialization. During the next 6 months the child develops a sense of empathy in relationship with peers, parents, and teachers and is taught the meaning of justice and the expectations of society. Most of the problems of society could be corrected at this state if parents and teachers operated through tough love to adjust attitudes and behavior. Much of the funds spent on the courts and prisons could be diverted to education. When a child reaches a higher stage of autonomy at about age 13, it is much harder to make the necessary corrections.

Since the data in the lower-level systems of the structure makes up the content of the higher-level, the system above a given level may be termed its *suprasystem* and should provide the information that teachers need to adequately evaluate students. *Subsystems* on the other hand, are systems within a given system. Most teachers are not sufficiently prepared to measure the subsystem components of an individual or to assess the aspects of intellectual capacity and/or support, and such mechanisms cannot be directly measured by standard tests. Since the individual is made up of organs and teachers normally do not have criteria to make judgments on the health of human organs or productive cell activity, most evaluations and grading are arbitrary or based on insufficient grounds. Education is not sufficiently equipped to deal with the organism-level because the data comes from the previous level.

LST Constructs and Education

All aspects of education, including administrators, principals, teachers, guidance counselors and aides are directly and obviously concerned with three levels of living systems, i.e., organism, group, and organization. Less directly, but quite obviously, they are also concerned about the level of community. Therefore, by the nature of their concerns, the family and social issues are cross-level disciplines. LST provides a handy set of vocabulary, concepts, and postulates in a logical framework to facilitate assessment of these issues through the consideration of the twenty (20) critical subsystems that relate to all living systems including the teaching/learning process.

Classroom teachers and tutors are interested in individuals (organism level). One cannot teach cohorts, classes, subjects, they can only teach individuals. It is appropriate then for teachers to be aware of the health and family environments of each student because full knowledge of a student's capacity cannot be assessed only by what occurs in the classroom. Personal health, living environment, diet and rest must be considered. The degree of parental or adult interest in the student's academic achievement is a critical part of classroom performance.

Notwithstanding that the teacher is teaching individuals, the class or cohort is important. Peer influence and group behavior impacts the performance of individual members of the group. Since understanding the group or cohort requires that data be gathered from the previous level, the organism (individual), the teacher must have relevant knowledge of each member of the class to adequately teach the subject. Individuals learn through personal discovery, but they also learn from each other.

Administrators and supervisors are concerned with the community level that is made up of groups. To provide adequate oversight to a school, the supervisors must have knowledge of all classes and cohorts as to curriculum, teacher competency, learning assessments, behavior, and the function of the teaching/learning process.

Since each level is understood by gathering data from the previous level, those who supervise school systems or groups of schools must be aware of the teachers, students, and parents. Also, they must be adequately informed about community organizations that impact the various schools under their supervision. The nature and stability of each community creates an environment that either interferes or enables the teaching/learning process of the school. Supervisors must be totally aware of local politics, the socio-economic level of the community, the presence of gangs, drug use, criminal activity, and the stability of the family units from which students come. All of these are vital to the proper function of a school and the assessment of achievement for both teachers and students. When comparing the data from a district or regional area, this information should be factored into the evaluation. Otherwise the teachers, staff, and students do not have a level playing field. An apparent example may expose the problem. Should teachers and students in one school with a negative community environment be evaluated weak while a school in a positive community is judged to be strong? It is obvious that such an assessment would be unfair. This can breed discouragement and loss of good personnel and further disadvantage students in their pursuit of higher education.

Critical Subsystems of Living Systems

The twenty (20) subsystems that process information or material-energy or both account for the survival of living systems, at any level. These subsystems are summarized below:

The twenty subsystems and processes of all living systems arranged by input-throughput-output

Processes in the Systems Input Stage;
- **input transducer** brings information into the system;
- **ingestor** brings material-energy into the system.

Processes in the Systems Throughput Stage
A. information processes:
- **internal transducer** receives and converts information brought into system;
- **channel and net** distributes information throughout the system;
- **decoder** prepares information for use by the system;
- **timer** (clock) maintains the appropriate spatial/temporal relationships;
- **associator** maintain appropriate relationships between information sources;

- **memory** stores information for system use;
- **decider** makes decisions about various system operations;
- **encoder** converts information to needed and usable form

B. material-energy processes:
- **reproducer** with information, carries on reproductive function;
- **boundary** with information, protects system from outside influences;
- **distributor** distributes material-energy for use throughout the system
- **converter** changes material-energy into suitable form for use by the system;
- **producer** synthesizes material-energy for use within the system;
- **storage** stores material-energy used by the system;
- **motor** handles mobility of various parts of the system;
- **supporter** provides physical support to the system.

Processes in the Systems Output Stage:
- **output transducer** handles information output of the system;
- **extruder** handles material-energy discharged by the system.

Since Miller's Living Systems Theory is a general theory, the listed concepts are allegorical only. With some depth of understanding, Miller's LST work maybe algebraically translated to concepts useful to education. This is based on an understanding that all living systems at each level possess the same twenty critical functional subsystems (see Figure 3.2.). This commonality is explained by the principle of "fray-out" (earlier termed "shred out"). The term *fray-out* is used to describe a sort of evolutionary specialization in which the higher-order systems evolved from the lower-order ones. While some of these functions may be upwardly, downwardly, or laterally dispersed to other systems, all functions (except the **reproducer**) must occur for a given living system to endure. This is why the subsystems are called critical.

List of the Critical Subsystems:

SUBSYSTEMS WHICH PROCESS BOTH MATTER-ENERGY AND INFORMATION
1. **Reproducer**, the subsystem which carries out the instructions in the genetic information or charter of a system and mobilizes matter and energy to produce one or more similar systems.
2. **Boundary**, the subsystem at the perimeter of a system that holds together the components which make up the system, protects them from environmental stresses, and excludes or permits entry to various sorts of matter-energy and information.

SUBSYSTEMS WHICH PROCESS MATTER-ENERGY – TEACHING *
3. **Ingestor**, the subsystem which brings matter-energy across the system boundary from the environment.
4. **Distributor**, the subsystem which carries inputs from outside the system or outputs from its subsystems around the system to each component.
5. **Converter**, the subsystem which changes certain inputs to the system into forms more useful for the special processes of that particular system.
6. **Producer**, the subsystem which forms stable associations that endure for significant periods among matter-energy inputs to the system or outputs from its converter, the material synthesized being for growth, damage repair, or replacement of components of the system, or for providing energy for moving or constituting the system's outputs of products or information markers to its suprasystem.
7. **Matter-energy storage**, the subsystem which places matter or energy at some location in the system, retains it over time, and retrieves it.
8. **Extruder**, the subsystem which transmits matter-energy out of the system in the forms of products or wastes.
9. **Motor**, The subsystem which moves the system or parts of it in relation to part or all of its environment or moves components of its environment in relation to each other
10. **Supporter**, the subsystem which maintains the proper spatial

relationships among components of the system so that they can interact without weighing each other down or crowding each other.

SUBSYSTEMS WHICH PROCESS INFORMATION – LEARNING *

    11. Input transducer, the sensory subsystem which brings markers bearing information into the system, changing them to other matter-energy forms suitable for transmission within it

    12. Internal transducer, the sensory subsystem which receives, from subsystems or components within the system, markers bearing information about significant alterations in those subsystems or components, changing them to other matter-energy forms of a sort which can be transmitted within it

    13. Channel and net, the subsystem composed of a single route in physical space or multiple interconnected routes over which markers bearing information are transmitted to all parts of the system

    14. Timer, the clock, set by information from the input transducer about states of the environment, which uses information about processes in the system to measure the passage of time, and transmits to the decider signals that facilitate coordination of the system's processes in time

    15. Decoder, the subsystem which alters the code of information input to it through the input transducer or internal transducer into a "private" code that can be used internally by the system.

    16. Associator, the subsystem which carries out the first stage of the learning process, forming enduring associations among items of information in the system.

    17. Memory, the subsystem which carries out the second stage of the learning process, storing information in the system for different periods of time, and then retrieving it

    18. Decider, the executive subsystem which receives information inputs from all other subsystems and transmits to them outputs for guidance, coordination, and control of the system

    19. Encoder, the subsystem which alters the code of information input to it from other information processing subsystems, from a "private" code used internally by the system into a "public" code which can be interpreted by other systems in its environment

    20. Output transducer, the subsystem which puts out markers bearing information from the system, changing markers within the system into other matter-energy forms which can be transmitted over channels in the system's environment.

Source: Swanson and Green, (1991). * The Teaching/Learning divisions are a recommendation of this book for reader discussion and application.

Figure 3.2–The twenty critical subsystems of all living systems

Bailey (2006) wrote that Miller's Living Systems (1978) was the "most integrative" social systems theory, and that LST made many contributions that were easily overlooked. My colleague G. A. Swanson applied LST to a general theory of accounting in his dissertation and this writer has applied Living System to social research for the past twenty-five years. It is assumed that some constructs of LST have relevance to education. (Swanson and Green, 1991) Some suggested constructs of LST with application to the teaching/learning process are listed below many more may be generated by consideration of dividing the critical subsystems into the categories of Teaching and Learning suggested above:

1. LST makes a distinction between (concrete) unsolvable issues and (abstracted) selected issues that could be addressed by a problem solver.
2. A LST concrete system represents many interactive and interrelated elements and is usually too complex to deal with as a whole. The first step is to divide the problem into two or more parts. Normally, there are two kinds of problems, (1) a problem to find an answer, and (2) a problem to confirm that the answer is the best one. Complex problems may need to be separated into many parts based on prior knowledge of the general subject.
3. The LST abstracted system consists of selected parts of a complex system or the abstracted parts of a concrete system. Based on prior knowledge those understood parts must be selected or abstracted from the system to make a solution manageable.
4. The LST conceptual system is made up of words, symbols, and numbers used in a declarative sentence to explain the abstraction or the selected elements of the concrete system that were selected for consideration.
5. The LST measure of the random errors (noise) that occurs in communications speaks to the learning environment
6. LST provides an innovative approach to structure–process issues that could easily be identified with the transactional distance in the learning process based on the level of structure. It emphasizes the interrelatedness of structure and process; such as, the greater the structure the greater the transactional distance in the learning process. This informs the teacher to lessen the structure and provide more individual freedom to enhance the learning process.

7. LST suggest a joint subsystem—a subsystem that belongs to two systems simultaneously. This could relate to the common ground between the teacher and the learner that forms a basis for learning in the teaching/learning process. Since the unknown is always learned based on the known, what the teacher knows and what the learner knows combines to create a learning activity that stores up information, facts, and data to be used to answer questions or solve problems in the present and the future.

8. LST constructs present various aspects of dispersal (lateral, outward, upward, and downward). This could relate to the thinning out of the ranks in education; as students proceeds up the ladder, the incompetent ones are removed through a kind of lateral arabesque. Educational leaders are moved from position to position until they reach a level of incompetence based on the Peter Principle. Also, the dispersal factor suggests the grading, social promotion, dropouts, and failure of students in the process.

9. Inclusion of something from the environment that is not part of the system when information, facts, or data are used to answer a question or solve a problem, knowledge is created and it is the evidence of learning.

10. The discussion of physical space and time is germane to the classroom because the clock is running on each class, term, year, etc. and what does not get done in the specified period of time can hinder the future development of each student.

11. The concept of artifacts which are man-made extensions speaks directly to computers, the Internet, and classroom teaching technology.

12. The adjustment process that combats stress is the essence of what a good teacher does in presenting a subject to a class.

13. LST also analyzes organizational abnormalities and suggests functions that are not normal (e.g., system stress and strain, feedback irregularities, information-input overload). These may be relevant to the abundance of content presented in the classroom that produces an information overload and the feedback on exams and essays are not acceptable

14. LST's analysis of the eight interrelated system levels, enables one to understand how social systems (such as, the classroom) are linked to the biological systems (of teacher and learner).

15. The twenty critical subsystems that carry out processes that all living systems need to survive and LST's analysis distinguishes between matter/energy processing and information processing. This analysis relates to the effort of the teacher to communicate

content and the listening, analysis, and action of the learner to
process the information presented.

A classroom teacher has two main concerns: the students
and the lesson. It is a constant balancing act to maintain
adequate and proportional concern for both in order to create
an environment conducive to learning. This balancing act is
similar to the concept of a Steady State System.

Living Systems Maintain a Steady State

By processing matter-energy and information, living systems
maintain themselves in a dynamic *steady state* of complexity
over time. In this context, the term steady state is defined in
relation to these three terms: (1) structure, (2) process, and
(3) state. *Structure* is the arrangement of a living system's
subsystems and components in three-dimensional space
at a given moment in time. *Structure* always changes over
time. *Process* is all change over time of matter-energy and
information in a system. It includes both *function* and *history*.
Function is reversible actions that alter structure succeeding
each other from moment to moment, while *history* is defined
as less readily reversible actions that alter both the structure
and the function of the system. *State* is the arrangement
of a living system's subsystems and components in a four-
dimensional space of time that always changes over time.
State must therefore be observed over some time period
and the critical information about steady state is defined
as a condition in which the changes in the relationships
between systems elements and between the system and its
suprasystem are maintained within relatively narrow ranges
over time.

CHAPTER FOUR

Maturity and Transformational Guidance

A Rearview Mirror

The Canadian writer, McLuhan (1967) assumed that mankind viewed the future through a rearview mirror. Students normally view a new educational environment through the perspective of a rearview mirror. They will attempt to evaluate the new teacher based on their experience with past teachers. If it were negative, normally a negative view will be the first impression. If the student experienced poor instructions in the past, it will be expected. If difficulty existed in following the instructions of a previous teacher and there was difficulty in figuring out what was on the test, the same may be true in the new experience. This means the first class and early days of a new term are important and all teachers must strive to be open, approachable, and believable. During the early state of classroom relationship building the instructor's behavior should be high task and low relationship. Most students want to know up front what is expected of them; however, this information must be provided in a user-friendly manner, without threats or the fear of failure.

Arriving in a new school or new class, a student will go through at least four stages: Form, Storm, Norm and Perform. In each of these stages there is a protocol for both task and relationship that must be followed to make the system work adequately. Each of these stages relate to past experience and a level of maturity, but the maturity is not always age-specific and is related more to intellectual capacity. This is where students must be cut some slack. There should be no intimidation or threat of elimination. The initial instruction should include confidence that each one will do well in the subject or class. Change creates conflict both physical and emotional. An attempt to understand the student's point of view based on background, age, present health and level of academic achievement. In order to create respect, students must have confidence in the credentials of the instructor, confidence in the subject and the general curriculum. This confidence is created by the early "telling" of the teacher in answering anticipated questions, normally expressed by the interrogatives: who are you, where did you come from, what are your qualification to teach this subject, what is your experience, etc.?

Adjustment is slow and at times painful to a new school, a new subject, or a new instructor. Moving though the stages may take five minutes, the whole first class or the first week, or perhaps the whole term: no one can predict. Each student and each class will go though these stages (1) Form, (2) Storm, (3) Norm, and (4) Perform in adjusting to the curriculum and the learning environment. It is a relational process.

FORM	STORM	NORM	PERFORM
M1	M2	M3	M4

IMMATURE ————————————————————————→ MATURE

Figure 4.1 – Stages of Maturity

The behavior of the teacher must change as students go through these stages. The instructor's first stage behavior is

(1) Telling (high task-low relationship). Normally, one would think the obvious would be the norm (high relationship-low task) but providing an agenda, introduction of the textbook or syllabus, explaining how assignments will be made, the testing procedure, and how grades are assigned are essential to initiate an atmosphere conducive to learning. All this will assist students in their transition into the new learning environment.

All attention given to students must be either age-specific or based on a maturity assessment and emotionally appropriate. When a student is in stage one emotionally, they are vulnerable and dependent; the teacher must "tell" them all the things they need to know so they can begin to feel the first stage emotion (1) "I need you." This is basic to the teaching process where students must attend with interest to the instruction of the teacher. The feeling of "need" on the part of a student is directly related to confidence in the teacher's competency and early behavior.

Telling is a cognitive process based on adequate communication. Selling is in the affective domain and requires the instructor to demonstrate a genuine interest in the subject and the student. Participating is the relational aspect of teaching where both the student and the teacher contribute to the learning dynamics and share in the excitement of learning. Delegating is assigning both responsibility and accountability to the student in relation to a learning activity. This whole process follows the three basic goals of teaching: (1) arouse a spirit of inquiry, (2) stimulate interest, and (3) get the learner involved. The primary role of the teacher is to facilitate the self-activity of the learner and, as a rule, tell them nothing they can discover for themselves.

The range of teacher/learning emotions in the classroom will be: (1) "I Need You!" (2) "I Really Don't Need You!" (3) "I Need

Myself!" (4) "We Need Each Other!" If one identified the stages above as 1, 2, 3, and 4, the response attitude of the student in (1) Form Stage is Dependent or "I need you!" (2) in Storm Stage it is Counter-dependent or "I really don't need you!" (3) in the Norm Stage it is Independent or "I need myself." And in the (4) Perform Stage the attitude is Interdependent or "We need each other!" At the perform state real interaction and learning take place. When the mind and heart of the student are readily joined to the intellect and wisdom of the teacher, the process of discovery and academic development is enhanced.

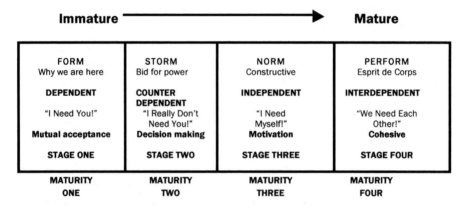

Immature ➜ **Mature**

FORM Why we are here	STORM Bid for power	NORM Constructive	PERFORM Esprit de Corps
DEPENDENT	**COUNTER DEPENDENT**	**INDEPENDENT**	**INTERDEPENDENT**
"I Need You!"	"I Really Don't Need You!"	"I Need Myself!"	"We Need Each Other!"
Mutual acceptance	**Decision making**	**Motivation**	**Cohesive**
STAGE ONE	STAGE TWO	STAGE THREE	STAGE FOUR
MATURITY ONE	**MATURITY TWO**	**MATURITY THREE**	**MATURITY FOUR**

Figure 4.2 – Stages of Learner and Class Maturity

Dealing with relationships is in reality dealing with the presence or absence of maturity. Maturity is more than age, it includes experience, responsibility, reliability, wisdom, and a general readiness for life as it comes. A mature person normally functions without excuses or blame and takes responsibility for their actions, deeds, manners, and general conduct. Maturity is not directly measured, but various items are assessed by surrogated evaluations. This may be more subjective than the system of education wishes, but experienced teachers develop an ability to make such judgments. The level of maturity is informed by past experience, development and a knowledge base. An awareness of maturity in the present is enlightened by wisdom, understanding, readiness, and capacity. Maturity also predicts the future through dependability, reliability and perseverance.

When one is dealing with individuals in a classroom environment, normally one does not see the acts or behavior of a mature person regardless of their age. A new subject and a new teacher create certain anxiety without respect to age or level of education. Making an adjustment to a different curriculum, different methodology, and/or different teachers and classmates can cause nervousness and apprehension. There is always the fear of failure and the desire to please the teacher and others.

At the **Form Stage**, the teacher must adequately inform the student of all opportunities and obligations related to the learning dynamics. The student is dependent on the teacher for guidance; therefore, they normally attend with interest to the instructions. When a negative reaction occurs it is called the **Storm Stage**. At this point the teacher must both tell and sell the pertinent issues to the student by stimulating interest and arousing a desire to discover new and exciting information. After the teacher has assisted the student to plot a course through the storm, the **Norm Stage** will immerge where the student clearly sees the value of the assignment and study requirements and comes to the realization that more knowledge about this subject is needed. Once the student reaches this level of participation, it is only a short step to the **Perform Stage** where students accept the delegation of responsibility and develop a sense of accountability for their performance. Now the teaching and learning process is working.

One fact remains clear in instructing students: they are individuals and each one is different. The Perform Stage is the goal, but students normally experience a learning rollercoaster ride with the transactional distance in the learning process ranging from an immature reaction to a mature response. Students go through all the stages: form, storm, norm and perform. In fact when a student is in the norm or perform stage, certain events cause their mind and emotions to reset to storm stage.

The antecedent cause of this occurrence is not fully understood, but it has to do with past experience determining a response to present stimuli. Knowing the stage of individual students and the maturity of a class at a given time is necessary for the teacher to determine an appropriate behavior: (1) **Telling** (high task-low relationship), (2) **Selling** (high task/high relationship, (3) **Participating** (high relationship-low task), or (4) Delegating (low relationship-low task). The behavior of the instruction leader normally follows a bell curve, and moves from telling, to selling, to participating, and finally to delegating. The learning activities are selected in response to the maturity and emotional level of a student or class at a given time and place. A closer review of the stages will improve an understanding of the process.

Stages of Teaching/Learning Process

The teacher's behavior follows the bell curve. Understanding the stages in the teaching/learning process will assist the teacher in developing positive outcomes. Relational and individual dynamics are prerequisite to effective learning outcomes with all students. Although the Cycle of Relationship Chart (Figure 4.2) primarily is about a more formal relationship building process, developing a growing friendship with a student is similar and one can learn from the chart. The process does not always go forward. Certain events or changes can cause a child in the Norm or Perform stage to reset to Storm stage. It is difficult to know all the things that create this plunge backward, but it happens. When it does, the caregiver must go back to Form stage behavior (Telling – High Task/low relationship) and move through the process again slowly.

Cycle of Relationship Chart

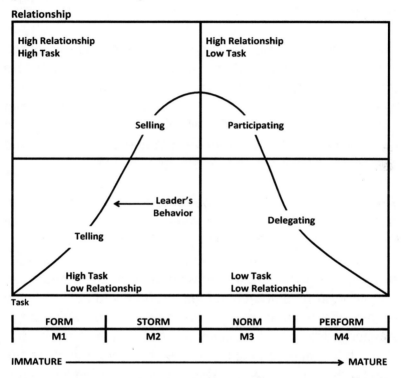

Figure 4.3–[M1-M4].

The teacher/leader's behavior follows a bell curve as an individual or a group matures: listed as [M1] Telling High Task/Low Relationship;; [M2] Selling, High Task/High Relationship,; [M3] Participating High Relationship/Low Task, and [M4] Delegating, Low Relationship/Low Task. Maturity is shown in four stages as MI, M2, M3, and M4.

Form Stage is a **dependent phase** for all students. There must be a mutual acceptance on the part of both the teacher and the student for the Form Stage to begin. The objective is a mutual responsiveness. At this point the teacher must establish rapport and find a point of secure attachment. This normally requires a conversation topic or activity that is of interest to the student.   During this stage the teacher is "telling" the student all the things that will lessen the mistrust of the learning environment. The teacher must be seen as a competent partner to create the "I need you" response which demonstrates that the student has accepted the first step into the learning process.

The "I need you" stage must have sufficient duration for the student to develop an interest in the subject at hand before the past presses the student to feel "I really don't need you" and attribute past failures and disappointments from previous teachers to the present class environment. When this happens it is the storm stage. Whether it is a gust of wind or a typhoon depends on the selling ability of the teacher

Storm Stage is a **counter-dependent phase**. The student is not certain the new environment and relationships will be beneficial. The dependent attitude was expressed as "I need you!" now the student feels "I really don't need you" and expresses this attitude through an emotional response. This is often modeled on something from the past, a failed subject or a negative style of teaching. The behavior of the teacher must be both competent and confident, but always high relationship and high task. During the storm stage the student is responding probably out of unconscious feelings erupting from past experience and needs to be sold on the advantages of knowledge in the subject. Also, the student must be reassured that the way forward is positive and the goal of completing the study is reachable.

First the teacher must respond with clear step-by-step guidance. It is possible the student did not hear or clearly understand the assignment. Patience is needed when a student is under stress. Nothing is gained in the teacher/ learner exchange when negative feelings remain entrenched in the emotions of the student. This is not the time for discipline. The student's behavior requires the teacher to add to the telling a kind of selling that motivates the student to move forward. Motivation is motive plus action. When the student's motive is understood, the teacher can provide an activity that the student is qualified to accomplish. This will place a "present-positive" in the subconscious to replace the negative response based on the past. During this counter-dependent phase, the student must see the benefits and positive outcome of the subject related learning activity.

Provided the student accepts the approach and makes a decision to move forward in a positive manner, the emotional response has been properly answered and the interaction becomes normal. During this stage the student is vulnerable and may remain unstable, this means the teacher must remain attentive and considerate. The best course forward may be to permit the student to take a step backward to the form stage where the response attitude was "I need you!" Then move deliberately toward the norm stage and the student has the emotion "I need myself." Then the teacher may participate with the student in the logical steps forward.

Norm Stage is a **participating phase**, a time when student and teacher can journey together in an agreed upon direction doing things that mutually benefit the learning process. It may take some time to reach the Norm Stage the process must not be rushed. This is when the student begins to mature into a self-directed mindset and is able to initiate learning activities acceptable to the teacher. Actually an independent relationship develops and the attitude becomes "I need myself." This is progress and a natural part of discovery and learning.

During this period of walking together, the teacher "participates" in the learning activities of the student and shares the excitement of the journey without intrusion or direction. The mode of operation is participation with the student in the learning process. This is a good place to be in the teaching/learning endeavor. This, of course, is accomplished in many different ways. An appropriate way forward must be selected from several options. To maintain the norm stage, the student's larger group relationship and the course of study must be considered and dealt with in a positive way. Students do not easily give up an unfair preference for or a dislike for a new teaching/learning environment that has not yet proven to be beneficial. This stage requires problem solving and positive sharing to move to an interactive attitude of "We need each other." Little progress can be made in the learning process until the student develops the "We need each other" outlook. This is the Perform Stage.

Perform Stage is an **interdependent phase** where the obvious attitude is "We need each other." Without the student, the teacher would be redundant. Without the teacher, the student would lack guidance and encouragement in the learning process. When this occurs the teaching/learning relationship is working. And an *esprit de corps* develops that enhances learning. A kind of "can do" spirit develops, and the student begins to self-actualize and the discovery process is opened further. When this occurs, the relationship has moved into the interdependent phase but needs additional effort to maintain. Normally, students are delegated to handle their own self-directedness with limited oversight by the teacher. This is a constructive phase, but most likely will not last. Something will happen or someone will unknowingly do something that triggers a retreat to the Storm Stage behavior of "I really don't need you" and an attitude of counter dependence. The process must be repeated.

Stages of Emotional Maturity

Previously it was stated that a stage could last five minutes, five hours, a week, or perhaps a term. In fact, a more realistic view of the form-storm-norm-perform process is not a static state but a steady state system. Different things cause the process to reset itself and repeat the steps. There will be many ups and downs depending on the maturity of the student. Even then it will reset to a place of comfort. This is dealing with the overall maturity of the student and the learning environment.

There will be times, places, and with certain people and subjects that a student demonstrates different levels of maturity. In other words, a student may develop a different timetable for each activity, event, occasion, or subject. An average student may go through the form/storm/norm/perform cycle many times on different occasions with different activities. It is the long-term timetable for adjustment to the teaching/learning process that is important. Be patient. Rome was not build in a day. It took the Creator six days to make the universe and then even the Creator took a day of rest!

When this process is understood, a teacher can adequately incorporate most students in their charge into the teaching and learning environment. Although there are time constraints in education related to class-time, term or semester dates, and assessment of outcomes related to a particular subject or course. It takes maturity and wisdom to make it work. The facts are that each student and each teacher may start each day at square one or the Form Stage. If so, simply go through the steps in the process of behaviors one at a time until the student and/or class reaches the desired level for each aspect of the subject and curriculum. An attentive teacher or learning leader can see the various emotional stages of the student or class moving from dependent, (I need you) to counter-dependent, (I really don't need you) to independent, (I need myself) to interdependent (We need each other).

In other words, these stages are not static. They are emotional stages similar to finding where pieces fit into a puzzle or points on a compass that the least variation in magnetism can cause the needle to point in a different direction. Instructing a class or teaching a student cannot be just "telling;" the teacher must get inside the mind and heart of students and see things from their perspective. To the degree a teacher understands the Form – Storm – Norm - Perform process, the more effective both teacher and student will become in teaching/learning dialogue and the greater the personal and professional satisfaction they will receive from their service in education.

Systematic Structure for Teaching/Learning

Based on assumption from the literature and decades of experience, custom, agreement, and/or formal and reasoned authority, a list of assumptions has been formulated for the study of the teaching/learning process. A great deal of systematically organized knowledge exists in the field of education and learning. Statements in the field differ based on basic assumptions or conjecture of the individual or discipline involved in the report; however, the assumptions are based on decades of experience together with agreed upon customs. Academics, superintendents, principals, lead teachers, classroom instructors, teacher's aids, and students have contributed to this experience base. Sadly, most of the literature neglects the early moral and ethical foundation that informs some of the key constructs that guide the teaching/ learning process.

Some call this set of rules or principles, established by custom and agreement, "laws." Others see the rules as a set of guidelines or statements devised to explain some phenomenon or class of phenomena and classify the list as "theories." Still others see the rules as self-evident or universally recognized facts that are accepted without validation and identify the list as "axioms." The following are simply worthy postulates or principles for the study or practice of the art or discipline of teaching and learning.

Here is a list of conditions that inform teaching/learning process. Call them axioms, theories, conditions or principles, they are all based on basics conditions. A rose by any other name would smell the same. Those in the trenches should do the judging.

Seven conditions govern contingency or situational development that may be used as predictors for easing the difficulty of choosing the correct approach, behavior, or structuring to make the teaching/learning cycle effective and move toward maturity.

Condition One
All students, classes, and groups begin at the Form stage.

Condition Two
In order for a student, class, or group to move from immaturity to maturity there must be a tutor, a teacher, or a leader.

Condition Three
The student, class, or group must have internal agreement that the subject at hand is worthy of their time and energy and has value for their future. Otherwise the teaching/learning output will be minimal and there will be little movement toward intellectual growth.

Condition Four
If the tutor, teacher, or leader fails to demonstrate present and future value of the subject at hand there will be no progress in the teaching/learning process. Classroom dynamics may force the issue through grades and rewards, but these artificial

stimuli are of little value to future learning. If those in charge determine a lack of interest in the subject or task at hand, a change in the leader's behavior may change the action in a positive direction.

Condition Five

The teaching/learning process will reset towards immaturity when one of the following occurs:

1. **When new individuals are added** to the students, class or group mix, normally there will be a reset to the Storm Stage until the function of the new members is defined and any conflicts are removed. Teaachers must be prepared for such contingency and return to a "telling" mode of high task – low relationship to assimilate new members and bring the group together.

2. **When the tutor or teacher changes** it virtually constitutes a new subject, a new class, or a new group. The new leadership must start at Form Stage (high task-low relationship) and tell exactly why they are there and exactly what they are going to do. There must be no speculation as to "why the change" or "who the new person really is." Drastic changes by the new tutor or teacher will hinder the progress toward maturity.

3. **When the task changes** or a new class begins, a new activity is started, a new subject is initiated there will probably be a reset toward immaturity. This is where true leadership qualities are needed in a tutor, teacher, or group leader. Again, Form behavior is required to explain the reasons for and the advantages of the task change. Otherwise, there will be some passive-aggressive behavior where the intent is to do the least amount possible to meet the minimum expectations of the task at hand.

4. **The atmosphere, environment, or setting changes** such as moving to a new school, a different classroom,

returning from a fire drill, or anything the interrupts the interest and attention of the individuals involved, there will be reset toward immaturity. The person in charge must demonstrate Form behavior immediately to gain control and move the group forward.

In these reset examples, the degree of reset varies according to the original maturity of the student, class, or group. The more mature will recognize the reset and compensate by coming to grips with the change in order to return as quickly to the task at hand. The new member will be welcomed and the change embraced and movement back to a more mature stage will follow.

Condition Six

A sudden change in the behavior of a tutor, teacher, or leader has the same effect as changing leaders. Consequently, when this change is recognized the behavior of the leader must become Storm Stage (high task-high relationship). If the situation deteriorates the person in charge must move to Form Stage (high task-low relationship) to refine the task and reset the perimeters and/or boundaries of the process.

Once form–storm–norm–perform Cycle is understood, the correctness of the assumptions is reinforced daily. For example, a quick diagnosis of an upset group when frustration or confusion is demonstrated; it is obvious the stage is Storm and the high task/high relationship behavior is required. Should a group need better guidance, direction and understanding of the task at hand, the correct behavior is Form Stage (high task/low relationship) to establish movement toward maturity. This is possible even with an emotional response to an undesirable task.

Condition Seven

Common sense demands that a teacher's behavior be

governed by the needs and maturity of students. Common sense demands that tutors, teachers, administrators, counselors and all leaders use common sense. Yet, there is not enough common sense to go around.

CHAPTER FIVE

Understanding and Learning

Rethinking Education

Education involves ways and means of communicating information, facts, and data that may be used to answer a question or solve a problem, but these are not shared on a level playing field. The present grading system does not compare equals because of the variables that exist in the lives of different students and the arbitrary nature of exam construction and the subjective nature of student answers. The true essence of education is more than communication; it includes understanding the background and the environment in which teaching/learning occurs. Education establishes a feedback system for learners to answer questions, write essays or participate in discussion to demonstrate an understanding of subject content together with an attempt at application.

A student may demonstrate a limited understanding of the subject matter and a capacity to utilize the essential elements learned, but may not provide sufficient data to establish a fair and equitable assessment of either capacity or knowledge. Since learning and application are central objectives of education, why are students given a lower grade even after the facts are known? When the teacher explains the correct answer and a student discovers why an answer was not adequate, they now know the required information. Why should they be punished for not knowing it one hour before? In reality, those who know the answers before the test may be given a higher grade for memory, study habits, and learning skills, but those who learn the answer following the exam also know exactly what the teacher wanted them to learn. They may be rewarded with a slightly lower grade but should never be considered a failure. If pass-fail is the objective, why are grades awarded based on the "time" a student learned the information. Since all the correct answers are now know should a student not be rewarded with a grade that reflects their present knowledge of the subject? Transformational consideration is needed in the grading system.

Students begin a particular study at separate levels of achievement. Since all students in the classroom are not equal, there should be proportional grading system to both encourage the weak and cause the wise to use more of their capacity in the future. Why should a student take home a grade that does not reflect present knowledge? Students live in diverse environments and have various degrees of parental or adult intellectual encouragement and possess different levels of academic capacity. There are differences in general health, nutrition, rest and self-image. All these factors should be considered in a proportional grading system. Using the quiz as a written review and a learning tool is a fair system to both the student and the teacher because it also informs the teacher of the quality of their instruction without the obvious negativity.

A story from a missionary to India may shed light on the ranking or grading system. It seems two brothers were in the same school where the British system of ranking students top to bottom by numbers was practiced. When the brothers came home with the ranking list, the older boy was unhappy because he was number two on the list for his class, but the younger brother was excited when he was third from the bottom in his class and exclaimed to his father, "But there are two more bottom than I am!" Some students want to be at the top of the list while others are satisfied not to be on the bottom. This is part of the challenge of being a teacher.

Out of a laundry list of things a teacher wants students to learn, different students learn different things. This happens because all students are different with differing backgrounds, foundations, learning styles, and recall mechanisms. For example, a teacher wishes a student to learn many things during a subject or term and constructs an arbitrary quiz covering one-third of the concepts, ideas, or constructs. A student who was unable to articulate many of the selected constructs the teacher thought were important may still know many of the remaining concepts. These were added to a personal knowledge base and could be utilized in the future. Why the difference? Some things that are significant to teachers may not be important to the life-application of a particular student. The teacher must find ways and means of "teaching" these constructs also.

A teacher may know intuitively that certain students or a particular class of students are less informed on a subject than another because of a numerical test scores. Some teachers are less competent and have less experience than others. However, a quiz does not directly measure learning or capacity because testing and grading procedures are not adequately defined in education. Knowledge cannot be directly measured it must be assessed based on various criteria. The strength of this assessment lies within the ingenuity of the teacher's defense that the quiz questions constitute sufficient data to make a fair judgment on the student's learning or capacity. On the other hand, if the district or state stipulated a particular level on a standard examination, the score may represent sufficient criteria to evaluate the teacher but not necessarily sufficient information to assess learning or intellectual capacity of the student. Low scores by students may indicate weakness in the teaching rather than a lack of capacity in the students. A transformational system should be initiated to better assess both teaching and learning.

Understanding Grading

A bright student once asked a teacher, "What does the letter grade on my paper mean?" The teacher did not explain the strict counting of points normally used in assigning a grade, but gave a subjective answer that demonstrated a personal perspective.

- "A" means the work is acceptable for us both.
- "B" means you could do better and you know it.
- "C" means you were careless and we both know it.
- "D" means the devil is in the details and the future is dark.
- "F" is never used because failure is not an option. A teacher must tutor each student until they reach an adequate level of competency.

[Students scoring below a 'B' requires remedial tutoring. It is suggested the grades (C, D, and F) be combined into "TR" meaning Tutoring Required or "XT" meaning an extension for tutoring.]

This answer gave the student another way to look at grades. It is best to view an exam as both a content review for the student and a competency assessment for the teacher. The ability to communicate content in an interesting manner is a basic requirement of the teaching profession. When the teaching/learning process works, content is communicated and students learn sufficient amounts to satisfy basic grading requirements. When there is no learning, there was no teaching; therefore, poor performance by students may also mean poor teaching. If most of the students received the content and were able to reproduce the essential elements on an exam paper or in an essay, then the instruction was adequate. If only a few are unable to recall the content covered by the exam, then the teacher must look into other elements relative to the individual students. An exam or an essay should not be the only means to evaluate a student's academic achievement; they are only a part of an overall assessment of academic performance. Parents, home life, food, and friends should all be a part of the evaluation.

It may seem unconventional, but there are times when a "C" student should be given a "B" grade to encourage them on their academic journey. This should be based on an overall assessment of the student and not only on an exam or an essay. Also, there are times when an "A" student is performing below their potential and should be given a "B" to make them aware that they are performing below their capacity and need to press toward improvement.

Although "caning" is not an acceptable tool in modern education, it was a past form of correction administered to schoolchildren. The procedure of making a student aware of performance below their capacity is a good practice. This writer was witness to the outcome of an incident of "caning" many years ago in Jamaica, seated on the porch with the father of a student about 10 years old when his son came home with a troubled look on his face. The boy went straight passed us without speaking and the father got up and followed him into the house. When he returned he casually shared, "My son got his first caning today." Then he explained, "He dropped his homework on the way to school this morning and turned in a soiled paper. So the teacher gave him a few licks." This disturbed my "teacher's heart," but the father continued, "This is the best thing that could have happened to him. He had become careless about homework but will always remember the importance of not only doing homework but presenting it in an acceptable form to the teacher.

Somehow this concept of applied discipline for poor performance should be utilized, if not the physical aspects, then the emotional component could be used to call the student's attention to poor performance. A grade mark down together with remarks about functionality below potential may accomplish the required awareness. This could make a difference in future achievements. Historical records show that early in his education, Winston Churchill was "caned" when he did not perform up to his potential. The record shows that he became a real achiever. The physical punishment is not the issue, because just being made aware that he was capable of more might have made a difference. Perhaps this awareness is the responsibility of both teachers and parents if students are expected to reach their full capacity.

Many Old Rules Persist

Many of the old rules still apply, but a new road map for leading students into a better educational environment is being developed. Leaders in education must create and maintain a focused yet caring environment for learning. Leaders must know their personal strong and weak points and the strengths and weaknesses of others on their team to create a more effective learning environment. Everyone has weak areas and leaders make a big mistake when they become preoccupied on weakness without recognition of strengths. Weak areas should not be overlooked, but must be managed. And the best way to manage weakness is to concentrate on strengths. This can drastically increase commitment to the objectives and the achievement of goals advanced by learning leaders. Sufficient understanding of the weak areas of students can guide teachers in assigning work based on the strengths of all students and dealing personally with the individual weakness of a student.

Structure and Distance – Dialog and Support

The greater the structure in the learning environment the greater the transactional distance will be between the learner and the learning process itself.   Mature students may learn on their own, but this type of learning has not be prescribed or recognized in the past. Formal education requires interaction between the learner and a learning leader around structured curriculum. The conception in the field of education is that formal learning transaction required directed faculty/student interaction. This is the same process that gives the "A" student credit for knowing the answers at the time of the quiz, but does not recognize the "C" student who learns the answers after as a result of the test. When the "C" student discovered the unknown facts after the test most formal educators do not want to recognize this as part of the education process. If the quiz were seen as a written review, perhaps attitudes would change. Is not all learning based on self-discovery? Transformational thinking may reduce some of this prejudice as to the "the time and place" required for learning and thereby improve the teaching/learning process.

Could it be that the intolerance against informal education has softened in recent decades? Although the disapproval of the highly structured correspondence material remains because there is no room for dialog and support, the resistance has weakened for the more interactive ways and means of reaching and teaching learners. It appears that the limited classroom models of Europe particularly the Oxford/Cambridge (Oxbridge) model have increased the awareness that decreasing the structure may actually increase the learning. Also, that reading and research uses the authors of books as a source of dialog and support has increased the value and volume of informal education. The classroom model's increased quantity of homework may indicate a realization that much learning takes place outside the formal classroom. Obviously the current technology and newly developed mechanisms permit dialogue and support by a learning leader outside the formal environment. This virtual classroom concept is transforming the entire field of education. Even the very young are learning and using computers, and more mechanisms have been brought into the learning environment.

Many have become aware that the rote recitation of material year after year by a teacher may be worse than the old correspondence method for a large class of students. The only interaction is the passive student in silence takes a test and a teacher with limited interaction often without a word of explanation "grades" the paper with red ink and negative remarks. If such examinations are not used as written reviews and discussed with the student, in reality the learning value is weighted on the negative side. Classroom teachers of the young and immature student must be interactive and deal with the deficiencies of each student or learning fails and students are left behind.

Transactional distance is the sense of distance felt by the learner in a particular educational environment. Increased dialog and support also increase the learning. Moore (1973) defined transactional distance in terms of two factors: dialogue and structure. Dialogue is the teacher/ learner two-way communication. Structure relates to the adaptability of instructional components and methodology to the needs of the learner. Beder (1985) defined structure as a function of the formality of the subject matter. Dialogue decreases transactional distance and structure increases the transactional distance. As the structure of the learning situation is increased, more dialogue is needed to lessen the transactional distance.

Maturity in a student is not age-specific; however, there are no age minimums or maximums on learning maturity. When students, regardless of age demonstrate the mental, emotional, or physical characteristics associated with a well developed individual, they should be considered a mature learner with various degrees of autonomy. Learner autonomy is another vital dimension of the learning process among mature learners. Mature students are normally emotionally independent, self-motivated, and capable of coping with learning problems with a minimum of teacher assistance. Traditional education has fostered dependency throughout the secondary/tertiary education or the K-l2-College cycle; consequently, the restoration and support of the mature learner's autonomy is essential. A focus on problem-related topics is necessary to activate the mature learning process because most mature students learn primarily in relation to the life problems. Teachers and learning leaders must treat mature learners as autonomous learners.

Structure as a Function of Learning

Dialogue, structure, and learner autonomy are foundational elements in understanding learning. Dialogue should be seen as support for both aspects of the teaching/learning process. It must not only be a way to get answers concerning methodology or content, but it must be seen as emotional support for the learner. A high dialogue methodology is essential to maintain the attention of mature learners.

Structure as a function of the formality of the subject matter suggests the need for specialized competence in a field. This is a situational attribute (Pratt 1988) based largely on the learners personal knowledge and expertise. Instructors and tutors must consider the learner's situational attribute in the area of specialized competence when dealing with a learning transaction and in structuring the learning activities and environment. Dialogue becomes a means of determining specialized competence and a guide to adjusting structure to meet the needs of the learner.

General and Specialized Competence

General competence defined as self-directedness by Verduin

and Clark (1991) is not adequate to determine specialized competence. Skill in discussion, verbal discourse, or the ability to write well is not sufficient evidence of competence. The learner must be able to read and deal with additive and variant material, differentiate important and unimportant data, and record the meaning of important data in their own words in an abbreviated form.

As students advance through a course or through grade-levels, both general competence and specialized competency are required. A high-structured field such as mathematics requires more specialized competency on the part of the learner than a low-structured field such as social studies. Overview or entry-level courses require the least specialized competence. A strong foundation in general competency may enable a mature student to gain a great deal of specialized competency on their own.

Theories focus on learning in the ideal world, but learning takes place in the real world of family and community, politics and government. All this must be factored into the structure of the teaching/learning process together with learner autonomy, the degree of dialogue and support, the level of structure and specialized competence, and general competence and self-directedness. Teachers in advance or gifted programs tend to over generalize the nature of learning. This is done on the basis of mature learner theories and other general philosophies that relate to advance subjects.

Assumptions about Learning

Learning is an active process and most students prefer a participatory process in education; consequently, education must be filled with learning activities that are user friendly. Learning is a goal-directed process, but all students are not goal oriented; therefore, the clearer and more relevant the stated outcomes are the more learning will occur.

Class-based activities and group learning experiences must be done in an atmosphere of mutual learning and support for immediate and practical application. This becomes prompt reinforcement and constructive feedback. The early use and/or application of material learned places the information in the long-term memory and reinforces the recall ability of the student. All learning must be integrated into the daily life and future career of the student. The information directly applied to life greatly enhances the learning and recall process. Much content is forgotten, even though the process is remembered. The practical application of what is learned becomes a marker for recall similar to a file on a computer. When the marker is remembered the data can be retrieved and utilized many times. Useful data placed in the long-term memory is the goal of all education. This requires immediate application and reinforcement. When one uses information recently learned, the process of recall is strengthened.

All individuals have learning plateaus that require a period of reconsolidation. It is normal and students should be encouraged to work through any such difficulties. In fact the learning plateau is simply a mechanism of the memory to sort out all the data and place it in a useable place. At times learning cannot be rushed. Reflection time is of great value in the process of retaining what is learned. Learning is experiential but it is also logical as to subject matter and the facts must make sense in relation to the learner's past experience, present need and future goals.

An elective process is always helpful, because students learn best what they want to learn. Options in assignments and opportunities to demonstrate competency in projects are better than the traditional exam. Students should be given choices as to how they would demonstrate competency in a given subject. The methodology should permit learning logs, essays, papers, projects, a practicum, an internship, academic reports, research projects, and any other practical or theoretical process that could be determined to be useful to the active learner. Just as no child is the same as another in past experience, expertise, family life, health, religious convictions, because both past and present conditions impact the way students learn and demonstrate competency.

It should be remembered that good students have specific time-span and learning periods. In the United States for example, the odd years (grades) of schooling, 1,3,5,7,9, and 11 provide new material that is used in grades 2,4,6,8,,10, and 12. If the curriculum is based of sound educational philosophy and becomes a vehicle to carry the student to the next level, the odd and even is true of college years also. First year freshmen are prepared to become second year sophomores. Third year juniors are prepared to become seniors and them move on to higher education or into the job market. These periods factor into both the ability to do and the desire to do academic work. Learning for learning sake is probably not an option. All students should know that there is purpose to what and when they learn certain content. Most students do not store up information for possible use. They acquire knowledge to use this knowledge to advance their state and status. Only data with present usefulness is placed in the long-term memory. Only retrievable data has long-term value. These facts must be placed in the curriculum and teaching strategies for all age groups.

Cognitive Learning Theories

Cognitive learning theories may best describe pedagogical study. In such cases, teachers are an expert source and the learners are passive recipients of information. Andragogic learning situations may best be explained by the social sciences in which the students are more capable of self-direction and the teachers are more facilitative and directive. The individuality of mature learners must be recognized before an adequate learning experience can be designed.

Learning Styles

Learning styles have implications for teaching styles. Smith (1983) suggested certain tendencies and preferences of students influence their learning styles and the way they engage an educational experience. The individuality of learners regardless of age must be recognized before an adequate learning experience can be designed. The variety of background, home environment, general health, and past educational exposure complicates the process of education. Diversity in individual needs, goals, motivations and time must be recognized. Teaching strategies should not be of the "cookie cutting variety" but should take in to account the ways students prefer to receive information. Some students prefer to work with numbers, but others prefer to acquire new information through listening, reading, viewing or through the process of direct experience. Eight factors identify the preferred learning conditions; (1) **Peer work** (working in teams); (2) **Organization** (logical and organized course work); (3) **Goal setting** (setting one's own objective); (4) **Competition** (wanting a comparison with others); (5) **Instructor** (having a good rapport with the instructor); (6) **Detail** (wanting specific information on assignments); (7) **Independence** (wishing to work alone and independently); and (8) **Authority** (desiring classroom discipline and maintenance of order).

See Figure 5.1 on the following page:

Teacher and Classroom Learning. The numbers 1.1 – 9.9 relate to "concern for the student" and "concerning for the Lesson" 1.1 would be low concern for both while 9.1 would be high concern for the student and low concern for the lesson. This diagram normally used in leadership studies can easily be adapted to the teaching/learning process.

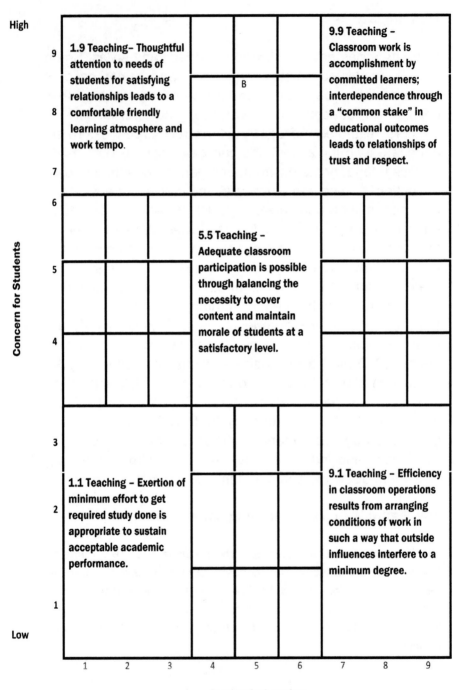

Concern for Learning

Low   **Figure 5.1**   High

The Planning Cycle

Finally, after leadership has used each opportunity to advance the mission of an organization in the direction of the purpose should time be given to solving problems. Before the planning cycle is restarted that deals with planning for the future, leadership must make corrections to the inferior process. Once an analysis of difficulties is made, leadership can begin constructing a superior process to move the organization forward. This planning process will result in a revision of both methods and policy. **Policy is answers worked out in advance for anticipated questions.** Methodology includes the approach one takes to answer all unanswered questions and the course of action required to move the organization toward the stated goals. Leadership must remember that one may not construct a superior process until the inferior process has been corrected. The proper order: correct the inferior then construct the superior.

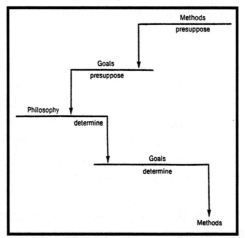

Figure 5.2 – Philosophy determines Goals determine Methods

All planning should have a foundation in philosophy and permit the philosophy to provide guidance in selecting specific goals. Once the philosophy and goals are joined, one can determine the methodology. It is tragic for a system to copy the methods of another system without clearly understanding the reasons behind the methods. The planning for educational delivery depends on the order of philosophy-goals-methods, and the relationship of these three, together with the maturity of the learners involved. The teacher must adjust to the maturity level of the learner to accomplish the educational process. The process is simple: First, it is a Telling activity. This leads to the necessity to Sell the subject to the students. Next comes participating when the teacher excites and directs the self-activity of the learner and gets the learner involved in the discussion. The simple goals of the teaching process are: 1) stimulate interest, 2) arouse a spirit of inquiry, and 3) get the learner involved. With this admonition: the teacher must excite and direct the self-activity of the learner and normally tell them nothing they can learn for themselves. Learning is in fact the process of discover.

To take advantage of the stage evaluation process as well as providing students an overview of the curriculum direction and ultimate goal, many educational programs utilizes a Two-track Plan (CPM-PERT).

Critical Path Method (CPM): This method works backward from a perception of the completed project. CPM is used in construction when a builder views both an architect drawing of a completed building and a set of working drawings of how the building is to be constructed. The builder, with a clear view of both plans and a conception of the finished product, establishes a target date for completion.

Working back from the target date, the builder considers time, material, and contingencies to establish a construction schedule. At this point the builder must start at the beginning, structure the building in stages, and arrange for an evaluation process based on the architect's plans. Each aspect of the construction must be done in sequence with the timeline affected by the duration of each stage. With the CPM the builder may evaluate progress in light of the terminal target data.

Performance Evaluation Review Technique (PERT): Each aspect of a project is viewed in the light of prerequisites. As each stage is satisfactorily completed, the project moves to the subsequent stage until the project is completed. Without the Critical Path Method time- line, the performance evaluation review technique cannot remain on schedule. It takes viewing the project from both the beginning and the end together with the sequence of stages to complete the project without loss or waste.

Total Life Perspective

All guidance and counseling must have a total life aspect. Bad conduct is related to a cluster of things. Most students can perform adequately in class provided they have a stable home environment, adequate rest, nourishing food, and the positive guidance of parents or guardian. Guidance counseling is not only related to the academics and conduct on the premises; it is related to the whole future of the student. What happens in school does not stay in school; it is recorded and becomes a part of the permanent record.

The end must be considered from the beginning. In most educational programs, students interface the curriculum in stages and may not understand or consider what the next step will be. This is a flaw in the system. Future objectives and goals should always drive education. When the long-range future is not considered, students cannot plan their life or career until the final stage is completed. This is not even good educational philosophy for the early stages of elementary and secondary education, because in the early years students are storing up information and facts for future use. The difficulties in math and science can be traced to the student not realizing how these studies would assist them in the future. It is true that the early vocational ambitions of children are not predictive of their adult profession, but it does teach them to think about the future and that is a healthy process in education.

A failure to view the future is also explanatory of many of the behavior problems of children. Provided young girls were taught the purpose of their god-given female equipment and that it had to do with marriage and motherhood, many of the moral problems would be solved. If young boys who are taught to respect their mother and sister, were taught to respect the girl next door and that someday she would be someone's wife and mother, some of the sexual freedom could be brought under control. If all students were taught that their behavior and grades in school would follow them all the days of their life, things might be different. It is worth a try.

The public record is for all to see. Bad conduct during the school years can literally be a monkey on one's back the rest of their lives. The record of academic achievement also is ever present to enhance or haunt the individual throughout life. All guidance counseling must deal with the total life perspective. The future does matter.

There is a record of a United States Senator announcing to run for President and his present achievements included earning a PhD in economics and being elected to high office did not keep the press from digging up his past. It seems that in his early education he failed and was required to repeat a grade. The press published this fact. His failure in early education came back to haunt him in his mature years. He dropped out of the race for the Presidency. More recently, the academic Grade Point Average of George W. Bush was published when he was running for President. It appeared that he was more interested in extra-curricular activities than in the required academic subjects. Guidance counseling in the academic arena must include the element of the life-long record that will either help or hinder during the adult years. It is difficult for the young to see that far into the future.

Guidance should include aligning academic and talent strategies that drive the future achievements. Personal strengths and positive psychology must be used to assist an understanding that present academic achievement and conduct impact the future. Will the student have access to higher education based on academic performance? Will the student as an adult be qualified for and hired for the position they desire? Will the student be able to function as a professional in the future based on the quality of their academic and conduct record?

Guidance should be assisting students to find their personal strengths and use them to qualify themselves for future participation in society. If the student does poorly in math; it is not the end of the world. Many adults functioning well as adults were weak in math, but they used their strengths to compensate for other areas of weakness. Guidance counseling must take these facts into account when giving students advice.

Learning Activities

It is not the purpose of this book to provide detail suggestions for class assignments or specific information about homework, fundamental guidance for a generic approach to learning designs and activities that advance learning will be shared. First, the there should be general and specific assignments related to Developmental Readings from various sources, the library, the Internet, etc. where students with age-specific levels of capacity should read based on subject guidelines or course objectives to add to their knowledge and to find and engage variant material. Students should view the authors of the books and articles as "real people" and interactive at the cognitive level with the author's words. These readings should teach both source selection and the documentation of references. Students should be taught to paraphrase rather than copy directly and to group their findings in a narrative around the guidelines or objectives furnished by the teacher. Secondly, general assignments relative to the writing of essays should become a common practice at all levels of education.

An essay is a "first attempt" to express oneself on a subject. All students must learn to freely and purposefully express themselves in writing.

Reading and writing both teach the skills of practical journalism and classical rhetoric. The use of language in writing is perhaps the best evidence of thinking and learning. Teachers then may use Developmental Readings and Essay Development as vehicles for classroom activities and homework assignments. Learning by doing and personal discovery is the best plan to place facts, information, data into the long-term memory to be used to answer questions and solve problems.

Some school systems are overcrowded and teachers are on overload, but they do what they can with what they have and hope for the best. This may have been sufficient a generation ago when rural school children had little hope for the future and those who taught them did not see a way out of poverty or did not know how to teach them to climb the ladder to a productive life. In those days, students in the classroom felt them were in the "middle of nowhere" with no one to guide them forward. Their parents were poor, their house was full of underfed children, and there were little prospects for a productive life ahead for them. However, this is not the case in the age of television and the Internet. The poorest of children are exposed to the outside world and desperately seek guidance through the maze and up the ladder to a productive future. They are tired of reaching up and touching bottom; they want what all children want: to knock on the door of opportunity and have it open with a clear path forward. This is the challenge that calls for a new approach to education; the call is for transformational leadership in education at all levels and in every location.

The age of technology has changed the face of education. The youngest of the children come to the classroom with an advanced understanding of the world. They learn from books, videos, games, from television, from the Internet, from family and friends. Students are now connected through cell phones and the Internet to knowledge sources not even dreamed of when most teachers were their age. Their level of knowledge far supersedes what teachers remember they knew at a comparable age.

Not only do students come to the classroom with advance knowledge, their parents are better educated than the parents of their teachers. This means parents should be better resources than the previous generation. The dynamics of homework and classroom activities have drastically changed, yet some teachers hold tenaciously to the old system used in their own early education. Most seem to stubbornly stick to methods that did not work in the horse and buggy days. Most are unwilling to change and disconnect from past attitudes and procedures. This will produce another generation that cannot read and many who are unable to adequately support themselves. Some will require financial aid and other benefits from a government agency. Much of this was preventable.

The future can be better when the leadership in education rethink curriculum structure and instruction methodology and use the new information to produce better results. The focus must change from the welfare of the teacher to the wellbeing of the students. Somehow we must stop growing the budget to build a buffer between the supervision and the teaching/ learning process. Research data supports the proposition that dollars and cents can never replace common sense in education. Classroom teachers must have the freedom to teach to the needs of the student rather than teach for better test results. A change in test scores may satisfy the budget watchers, but it does not assure better teachers or more useful learning.

Distance education and the process of learning style mapping revealed many of the weaknesses in teaching children. One thing is sure the previous methods will not work in the modern classroom. Even the processes that are only a few decades old are ineffective in lessening the transactional distance in the learning process. Since learning is discovery, perhaps education should return to some basic understanding of the process, with the stipulation that some things have changed and some remain the same.

Acknowledge the Knowledge Base

Teachers in early education must acknowledge the existence of a knowledge base. The knowledge base is made of up the short-term memory of data used to create the long-term memory that produces competency based knowledge and effective learning instruction builds on this basic understanding. Creative or divergent thinking is not done in a vacuum. It depends on and uses a knowledge base. Since all learning proceeds from the known to the unknown, all teaching must take into account what the student already knows. Close observation of the creative thinking processes of children illustrates clearly the critical role of the knowledge base.

Children overtime develop a core competency baseline that feeds a knowledge base upon which they will construct most of the information in formal education and reading. At about age 7 or near the time when a child is ready for new and exciting information, the knowledge baseline should be in place as a foundation. After this time, most of what is learned is related to something they already know. The ability to read and write at an appropriate level is required to proceed further in the educational process.

Why do education specialists say that children should read at a certain level by the end of a particular school year? The linguistic and cognitive demands on children after the third year of school are drastically changed. During the first three years of school, instruction should related to learning to read and learning to improve comprehension, after this point a transition is made and students read to learn. This is why the knowledge base at age 7 is critical to the educational and functional future of a student. Time moves forward in one direction. Students who read and write below a core competency baseline are left behind as the "readers" move on. Without this competency base, students cannot negotiate the transition from reading narrative or storybook prose to the level of an expository or informational text that provides detailed description of issues or the commentary on a written text that discusses its meaning and implications.

Classroom teachers and aides must understand the change from learning to read to reading to learn. Early instruction and development readings and comprehension skills build the base for measuring competency against an age-specific standard. The more and better a student reads, the firmer the knowledge base becomes. Now the curriculum and instruction model must change to facilitate the reading to learn.

An active engagement in reading is the basis for measuring learning and age-specific competency. The ability to construct the meaning from the text is a learning process that is active, cognitive, and affective. Background knowledge and prior experience are critical to reading and developing this baseline for written expression.

The ability to read and write is a complementary process that brings balance to learning. The development of one improves the other. Reading and writing involve complex thinking and enhance social interaction essential to all stages of intellectual development. Consequently, more reading and more essay writing must be added to the curriculum to take advantage of the existing knowledge base of the student.

Instructors must understand the practical value and use of essay writing in education. An essay is not to only to check the knowledge of English grammar and spelling, but provide students an opportunity to freely express their knowledge on a subject and give the teacher an opportunity to evaluate their prior knowledge. The actual meaning of "essay" should guide the understanding of how to properly use the essay. The construct of "essay" comes from [Middle English *assay* and Old French *essai;* both meaning "to try, or attempt"] and from Latin *exagium* and Greek *exagion* both meaning "a trial or weighing." From this one learns that an essay is not an article for a referred Journal to be taken to pieces by an "egghead academic" but an essay is a first attempt to express prior knowledge and understanding of a subject. Essays become an evaluation tool.

A "red ink" or overly academic evaluation of an essay can discourage a student from providing the instructor with the needed information required to weigh their age-specific knowledge on the subject at hand. When a teacher does not understand the reason for the essay and uses it only to assess the student's knowledge against the teacher's knowledge who may have majored in the subject in college, it becomes a pretense to show the teacher's superiority and only points out the weakness of the student without acknowledging what they know. Teachers should remember a primary lesson in philosophy "One never reaches a positive conclusion beginning with a negative premise."

When an environment is rich with the experience of reading and writing with available resources and opportunities to learn from positive evaluation of essays and exams, a student has developed productive strategies that can be used in and out of school. Constructive evaluation of an essay or an exam paper can be a source of encouragement and create an excitement for learning. In fact when a student finds out why they missed a question or clearly understands the missing elements in an essay, they have learned what the teacher wanted them to know in the first place. Why then should this evaluation be expressed in a negative manner that could dishearten the student? Why not see the glass as half-full rather than half-empty? A positive evaluation of a student's work is similar to the learning that comes from an adult reading to a child. It is positive and productive. The competency baseline is moved forward and upward with positive stroking and sympathetic evaluation of essays and exams.

When parents and others read to young children and personally demonstrate an interest in reading, children first see that others have interest in them and then they learn to associate letters with the speech sounds they represent. Phonemic awareness is a step toward learning to recognize the whole word as a unit and thus develop construct recognition which is essential to learning and utilizing the knowledge base. Children need a variety of strategies to model and demonstrate reading knowledge and skills. All students regardless of age need opportunities to read and this reading process and competency should be monitored and evaluated in a positive manner that encourages the student to learn and continue to express on paper without the fear of failure or a negative response from a teacher.

When a student is deficient in reading and writing skills, it normally means limited exposure to new words, books, and parental guidance. This is not the fault of the student. Those who care about the child's future academic performance must take the time and provide the energy to do remedial work with the student; otherwise, the academic future is seriously jeopardized by difficulties in reading and writing.

Instruction in reading is an essential part of remedial education. Reading is the doorway to learning. It is through reading that students gain access to history, politics, literature, news, and information. Without the ability to read well, it is difficult to become an adequate achiever. Reading is power. It is critical for self-improvement, self-awareness, and self-determination and is related to self-trust. Not only does reading provide access to the world, it opens the door to the inner self and provides a confidence that permits trust in others.

When students are limited in the area of reading and written expression, they have limited choices in life. Research supports the urgency of early instruction in reading. Children in the bottom one-fourth of the reading continuum are more likely to fail or become an early drop out of school. Dropping out of school often means abandoning hope for the future or literally dropping out of life.

Student's Prior Experience Provides Power

References to prior experience and power permeate the theories of experts in education. Dewey (1938) declared that education was best accomplished through experience, particularly where past experiences were adequately related to future learning. In addition, education must originate from the learner's needs, thereby acknowledging the learner's power. Kolb (1984) clearly stated that learning occurred when experience was transformed into concepts. Knowledge, then, is the transformation of experience. Jarvis (1987) stated that the educator's role was to stimulate the process and the learner was to determine the content. Information, facts, and data alone are not knowledge. To become knowledge the facts, information, or data must be used to answer a question or solve a problem. Then and only then is it placed in the long-term memory of the learner. Prior knowledge is a strength-based asset to learning. Students, based on prior experience, have strengths that can enhance the teaching/ learning process. Educators who ignore this strength and discourage teachers from taking action essential to the learning environment become a detriment to students. All education begins with the individual. All students bring to the educational process certain strengths based on prior experience and this must be factored into both the curriculum and the teaching and learning strategies.

Understanding Power in Education

All institutions and organizations should to be analyzed in terms of power resources. According to Hardy (1986) a useful taxonomy of power would be:

1 **Positional or legitimate power**, achieved by virtue of the position held;
2 **Expert power**, achieved by one's undisputed expertise or indispensability; power in this sense is the ability to cause others to act in ways they would not otherwise choose to act by virtue of one's position, expert knowledge, popularity, resources or influence, according to the sources of power held. Each source of power is manifested through distinctive methods, used to obtain appropriate actions or patters of behavior. Expert power is exercised similarly, so that the power holder provides expertise or information in return for compliance. Persuasion can also be used by those with expert power, and is the method commonly associated with personal power.
3 **Personal or referent power**, achieved through popularity or charisma; those with positional or legitimate power are able to exercise personal influence through the handling of rules and procedures, which are accepted because of the authority of the powder holder's position in the system.
4 **Resource power**, based on the capacity to reward or punish by giving or withholding resources; resource power

is exercised through exchange processes, whereby the power holder offers rewards in exchange for compliance with certain guidelines.

5 **Physical power,** based upon the ability to persuade others; physical power is demonstrated through the exercise of personal strength.

Such analyses enable those with planning responsibilities to assess both the sources of power held by individuals and groups influential within organizations and the methods by which they are likely to exercise that power.   Assessment can then be made of the possible outcomes of current and/ or potential conflicts, and of the strength and direction of such trends. Administrators can then examine the likelihood that particular plans will be supported or resisted by those individuals and groups in pursuit of either overt or covert objectives.

The administrative/leadership process thus becomes the "art of the possible" - the assessment of strategies and tactics which will win sufficient support to succeed.   This involves the analysis not only of the potential resistance of identified individuals, but the possible coalitions that might form to resist the implementation of a plan.

Leadership goes further, then, by looking for ways to win over potential opponents and to weaken or prevent the formation of such coalitions.   Leadership depends on many things. One's background and experiences plus time, task, attitude, maturity of the group and the willingness of the leader to change behavior as the maturity of the group changes.

A major difficulty in leadership is that normally everyone who is elected, appointed, or volunteered to serve in a given position is classified as a leader. Calling everyone a leader weaken the true function of leadership and complicates the task of administration and management. Those who have positions have positional influence, but are not considered leaders unless they also have personal influence; that is, the ability to influence others to follow them voluntarily toward stated objectives. To call individuals who simply hold a position a "leader" is to discredit the people who actually influence a group to accomplish the tasks assigned to them. In fact, when elected individuals perceive themselves to be in a leadership position but do not understand the difference in positional authority and personal influence; such people will function in a manner that normally will alienate them from the group. This is caused by role conflict.

Role conflict comes in various forms. When a person has one understanding of a positional role, but others see the role in a different light, there is conflict. When others expect certain acts or performance from a position but the person occupying that position does not clearly see that performance as part of their "job description" there is conflict. Whether it is personal-role conflict, inter-role conflict, or intra-role conflict, it is conflict and this hinders the progress of any organization. It might assist the understanding of leadership to know that often leaders are not elected, appointed or in other ways named to a positional role; they simply assume the role of leadership because they have personal influence. A person in position must understand and utilize this influence for the advancement of the organization. Otherwise, it becomes a competition for position and power and that will destroy any organization.

Understanding the Learner

The process of creating discriminating learners can be achieved only through active learning methods. Key elements, in the educational context are the background experiences students bring to the educational environment. There is also a different perception of the relationship between students and the teaching staff. Anything that causes the learner to become dependent on the face-to-face instructions actually denies the opportunity to grow and develop in a manner necessary for further education and the demands of adult life.

Quality and quantity are mutually exclusive; increase one and decrease the other. There must be a proportional balance between these two elements to maintain a stable or growing state. Perfection is not the goal of education; learning is the true objective. Grading on the curve, or placing students on a normal distribution, or ranking as one would do in a contest, is counterproductive. Quality in education comes when students are free to search and learn and discover a way forward. This is learning and should be rewarded with marks of quality and words of encouragement.

Learning is a self-paced path to discovery. The joy of learning and the instant empowerment of discovery are the factors that activate the search for excellence and quality. Of course each teacher wants all students to do excellent work, but what is excellence? In old American Grammar School the teacher often gave the grade "E" representing "excellent." The word was used as a predictor to forecast the future potential for accomplishment. When the teacher saw that a student had the foundational understanding to find a way forward, the grade "E" was awarded. Education no longer awards the "E" grade, but the concept of awarding excellence is needed for the more advanced students. The experience, expertise, and maturity of the student are predictive of their finding a way forward. It is also easy to assume that all information learned will be used promptly. The system should encourage the search for excellence.

The Learner Dichotomy

There are certain expectations of all students. Mature students should be responsible, independent, in control, subscribing to an acceptable value system and accepting the consequences of one's actions. The list is neither complete nor systematic; this is why definition is required. Maturity is more than an age. The construct incorporates a range of concepts as a student moves through the system from a place of beginning to what could be called graduating o the next level and on to a time of commencement of a productive life and career. At each stage society acknowledges the individual has reached a new level of participation in society with certain rights and responsibilities. Another aspect is that the stages of learning development have little respect for age; this means that teachers must deal with students based on maturity not age. Producing a socially responsible and productive citizen must be the ultimate goal of education and this goal must be recognized in designing educational strategies for all age groups.

Learning and Understanding

Mezirow (1981) declared that learning led to understanding of the world, social relationships, and oneself. Because of this learning, the individual is freed from psychological, institutional or environmental forces. Education for Freire (1970) revealed the perceptual reality and, in so doing, became a liberating force. In doing this, teachers acknowledge that education is life-related. Consequently, the teacher needs a comprehensive understanding of the learner's environment, the relevant power relationships and their view of themselves and their world. This experience/knowledge base is required to make the process work.

Experiential Learning and Self-Directed Learning

Two concepts are particularly pertinent for classroom educators: experiential learning and self-directed learning. The first takes cognizance of the learner's past experience and the second recognizes the individual's need for autonomy. There are four common conceptions of experiential learning although it refers to a spectrum of practices and ideologies. (1) Experiential learning is primarily the assessing of learning from life and work experience as a basis for creating new upward routes in education. (2) The need to focus on experiential learning is a basis for change in the purpose, structures and curricula of educational opportunities. (3) A need to emphasize experiential learning is a basis for social change and community action. And (4) Experiential learning is related to personal growth and development that affects the increase of self-awareness and competency.

Central to experiential learning activities are student involvement, learner control, and the relationship of the learning task to real life obligations. While traditional learning focuses on a product and knowledge, experiential learning is directed towards the process. The end product may be increased understanding, subsequent change or a plan for the future. Essential to experiential learning is a significant experience which plays an instrumental role in the learning process. Situated between the initial experience and the subsequent outcome is some plan of mental activity, be it generalization, conceptualization or reflection. The end may be personal or practical means of empowerment.

Experiential learning should hasten social change, learning by doing, personal or professional development and/or increased competency in some area of life. It is directed toward a holistic education and assessment procedures should address each of the cognitive, affective and psychomotor domain dimensions. Baud, Cohen and Walker

(1993) developed five propositions to assist adult educators in developing effective experiential learning opportunities and to increase the integrity of the professional practice of faculty. (1) Experience is the foundation of, and the stimulus for learning. (2) Learners actively construct their experience. (3) Learning is a holistic process. (4) Learning is socially and culturally constructed. (5) Learning is influenced by the socio-emotional context in which it occurs.

Teachers as Facilitators

Teachers become facilitators in the process of self-directed learning. The educators operate as consultants; provide referrals and resource persons for the learner. The educators must establish an environment which encourages self-diagnosis, the formulation of objectives and the learner's ability for the design, implementation and continuation of learning. Teachers must conceptualize their roles as significantly different from the old classroom model and be knowledgeable of the learner's physical, psychological, social, and cultural orientation and function in an appropriate manner to enhance an atmosphere conducive to self-directed learning. The teacher's instructional and learning philosophy and subsequent teaching style obviously form crucial elements in appropriate interface with learners. From a philosophical perspective, both pragmatism and existentialism seem least at odds with self-actualized learning. The former has obvious advantages with its emphasis on observed reality and the latter because of its basis on reality as existence (Gutek, 1988).

An Organized and Sustainable Effort

Mezirow (1983) argued that the education should be an organized and sustainable effort to assist students to learn in a way that enhances their capability to function as independent learners. Provided a conducive climate exists and the student possesses the appropriate characteristics, teachers need to encourage the development of the identified appropriate skills. They are: (1) the capacity to define learning needs; (2) to be able to plan appropriate experiences; (3) to manage the learning situation; (4) to reflect upon the experience; and (5) to evaluate their own effectiveness.

Self-Paced Learning Model

Once these skills are attained, the student has the potential for progress through the learning steps of initiation, planning, managing and evaluation as a self-paced learner. The self-paced learning model promotes empowerment, relevance of learning, self-study, and cooperation with others. The grand prize question is why do students fail to persevere in education? Could it be because of certain blockages? Essentially, students fail to keep trying because there is no bridge between their present knowledge and the teacher knowledge.

When teachers fail to build a knowledge bridge between their content capacity and the learning capacity of the student, sufficient obstruction to learning occurs to block perseverance. Blockages occur because of a lack of emotional investment by both the teacher and the learner. Prejudices and bad study habits contribute to the failure. Experiential learning and, eventually, self-paced learning will minimize the likelihood that such blockages will occur. Matching instructional modality to the learner's needs is undoubtedly the most significant action that the teacher makes.

Teaching is Situational

What is good teaching for one student in one stage of development may not be good teaching for another student or even for the same student at a different stage of development. Good teaching does two things: it matches the student's stage of self-paced learning, and it empowers the student to progress toward greater self-actualization. Good teaching is situational, yet it provides the long-term development of the student.

The entire educational system is based on a growth development from high structure to little or no structure, from kindergarten to graduate work in which the structure or task is lessened and the relationship between teacher-leader and student-follower grows systematically less until the term for attending one of the acknowledged high seats of learning is to "read for a degree." This implies external tasking and requires self-actualization on the part of the student with limited, but valued input mixed with a dash of care and concern from the teacher.

Teaching Model

Transformational education models use interactive learning designs. Traditional pedagogic methods are used when they are necessary to instruct, tutor, or communicate specific content essential to academic advancement. Teachers must create an educational climate conducive to learning that promotes mutual respect and trust in the learning process. The intention is to develop an independent learner who has outgrown the need for structured guidance and has advanced to self-actualization.

In an effort to implement a self-actualization model of educational, one must understand both the dynamics of teaching and the change-producing forces of learning. The model provides a structure for students to acquire both content and competency to become a life-long learner. Students are encouraged to exercise initiative and personal skills relative to enhancing a vocational or professional direction. Teachers become truly effective when their students become achievers.

Curricular Structure

All educational programs should be structured to facilitate rather than intimidate. The educational process must not attempt to manipulate a student through constant threat of failure. The process is diagnostic and prescriptive in an effort to facilitate an acquisition of knowledge and move students to the next level of achievement. The student is expected to study the prescribed sources under the guidance of a teacher with continuous dialog and support. The basic goal is to excite and direct the self-activity of the learner. Student's work at one level is considered preparation for the next step on the educational journey.

Synergogic Methodology

As a sympathetic system certain teaching methods are sophisticated but not complicated. When one understands how the plan works it becomes less difficult. Knowing the needs of students in a learning environment is the difference. When one works with a sympathetic system, a working together develops that simplifies the process. Synergy occurs when two or more forces work so the combined effort is greater than the sum of the individual efforts. A sympathetic system requires knowledge of the system and an understanding of how the system works. Understanding requires both discernment and comprehension that permits a reconciliation of differences; thus, it becomes sympathetic. When students pool their knowledge on almost any subject, the combined subject matter is increased and individuals learn from one another. The saying may be true that "Two good students know more than one teacher, they just do not have the presentation skills that teachers acquire." At least, when students are given an opportunity to work together on a subject or a project, the level of knowledge and understanding is beyond expectation.

Structure and Distance

The greater the structure in education the greater the transactional distance the student is from the learning process. Distance in education relates to the degree the student is removed from the learning process. The goals of the teaching process are (1) to stimulate interest, (2) to arouse a spirit of inquiry, and (3) to get the learner involved. When the structure is lessened and students work together the transactional distance in learning becomes less and students learn more. Structure is used to both guide and limit the activity of the learner. The more complex and inflexible the structure the less the learner is involved in the cognitive process and the more the learner must rely on the teacher to "tell" or provide the content elements. To lessen the structure is to provide more opportunity for the learner to discover through the cognitive process the content elements of the subject.

CHAPTER SIX

Learner Maturity and Leader Behavior

Contingency Theory and the Learning Leader

Contingency theory is an assumption about an educational leader's behavior based on the maturity level of either individuals or the group. The model offers a choice of behaviors to a teacher that produces the best chance of influencing students to accomplish the task at hand. The contingency idea suggests behavior is dependent on change of factors that are presently unknown. As a teacher's circumstance or the maturity of individuals or a group changes, the teacher's behavior must change to match the situation. This assumption is a result of adding attitude to the mix or a teacher's predisposition to certain behavior based on changes in the maturity of students. Leadership is similar to the search for the Holy Grail it continues to search for new and workable assumptions about teacher and learner behavior. The most practical and workable assumption is the contingency/maturity assumption. This is true because it is derived from actual everyday real-life experience. It is natural to relate differently to individual of different ages and various levels of maturity and competency. No one has to explain the details or the difference of adult interaction with a three-year old, a 13-year old, a 30-year old, or a 60-year old individual. It is based on common sense.

Contingency leadership is an assumption based on work

done at Ohio University Center for Leadership Studies and the US Navy. It offers practical solutions to the basic problem of leadership behavior, based on given behavior of individuals and a certain level of maturity. Hennesy and Blanchard expanded on this theory by providing a conceptual framework to enable leaders to recognize certain behavior within a group and choose a behavior based on a combination of task and relationship that insured the probability of advancing the group or individual toward maturity.

Contingency theory or a kind of cybernetics suggests that students development towards maturity has four stages, each requiring specific behavior modification by teachers in order to achieve the most desirable perform stage. The assumption also suggests that the leader must make behavior modifications as individuals or the group matures. The critical part is that the leader must know what behavior to exhibit on a high-low continuum relative to task and relationships. It is not necessary for the individuals or the group to be aware of the changes in the leader's behavior.

A primary emphasis in the contingency or life-cycle assumption is on the behavior of the leader, but only in its relationship to the maturity of individuals or the group of concern. The assumption is based on curvilinear association between leader task and relationship behavior and group interaction, and provides an insight into the relationship between adequate leadership and the levels of demonstrated maturity. If there were no followers, leaders would be redundant. Individual acceptance or rejection of the leader actually determines whatever personal influence of positional power the leader may have with the individuals or the group.

A maturity continuum is shown and a task/relationship application to the leader's behavior. The key to adequate leadership is the determination of group maturity. Recognition of the maturity level of the group is vital. The leader must exhibit behavior of that is appropriate to this maturity. The maturity level of individuals within the group is also crucial to leader attitude. The appropriate leader behavior may easily differ for an individual in a group than for the group as a whole.

Individual and group response to the Task	"What's the task?" "Why am I here?" "Why are you here?" "I've got other things to do!"	Emotional response to task "I don't like it." "I like it." "Why do we do it this way?"	Roles defined Method of sharing resources worked out Work load divided and Coordination of work	Solutions to problems High efficient product Job done well with minimum effort
Relationship of individuals within the group	Testing, probing one another and leader Lessening the mistrust	Group checks leader's credibility if it doesn't like the task Polarization of group Cliques develop in groups Learning to trust others	Polarities and cliques dissolve Group begins to operate as a group Cliques and individuals begin to listen Begin to block out non-group members	Group energy focused on task Relationship taken care of automatically Relationship between members is supportive of each other and the task
Individual and Group Behavior	Mutual acceptance DEPENDENT	Decision making COUNTER DEPENDENT	Constructive INDEPENDENT	Cohesiveness/ Control INTER- DEPENDENT
STAGES	FORM Why we're here	STORM Bid for power	NORM Motivation	PERFORM Esprit de corps

IMMATURE...>MATURE

Figure 6.1 - Teacher and class behavior guide to maturity

Leaders must also note the data in Figure 6.2 on the following page. A clear understanding of this data will arm a leader with the mental resources needed to be adequate in any position. It is clear in marriage and group function that change in behavior is required to be equal to the present needs of either a partner or a group.

Model high	Allow emotional	Encourage	
Model high commitment to task.	Allow emotional response to the task to take place.	Encourage role selected by individuals.	Allow group to perform.
Set goals.			Encourage those things which prevent boredom.
State expectations	Identify the coalitions/ polarizations.	Encourage group consensus.	
Encourage disclosure of resources in relation to task.	Explain consequences and that they are unacceptable.	Roles may be different for short term focus than long, also for different environment.	Focus on environmental conditions which can be changed to produce more challenge.
Demand commitment and accountability.			
	Respond to credibility check honestly – don't punish.		Plan for the future.
		Take advantage of opportunities.	
	Negotiate an understanding or seek outside source to assist in moving block.		
	Maintain congruence and high concern for all members.		
High Task –	High Task –	Low Task –	Low Task –
Low Relationship	High Relationship	High Relationship	Low Relationship
MATURITY 1	MATURITY 2	MATURITY 3	MATURITY 4
FORM	STORM	NORM	PERFORM

IMMATURE...>MATURE

Figure 6.2 – Changes in teacher behavior based on class maturity

Another way to view the cycle of relationship is to look at marriage and the contractual-relationship that exists in this arrangement. The education/teaching process seems to go through the same cycle as other contract relationships (See Figure 6.3). All contracts are a compromise. This is not a bad word: note com-promise; it simply means "together" and "promise." It is assumed by this book that this interactive relationship works between teacher and student and that the teaching/learning process follows the same four stages: form, storm, norm, and perform.

CYCLE OF RELATIONSHIP

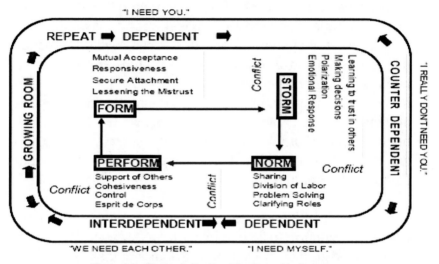

Figure 6.3– Stages in the Teaching/Learning Process

The assignment of students to a particular class and teacher is a kind of contract and has all the ramifications of agreements that must be kept to move forward with the positive advantages of the relationship. One agrees to give up something to get something. This is life and leaders must never forget that leadership of an organization is a true reality show. The phases or cycles are real and should be respected. When a leader understands the cycle or phase in which a group is operating, then the leader can stand firm without fear. It is the only way to survive in the organizational climate of the day.

Teacher-Student Relationship

Probably the most universal application of the lifecycle assumption occurs in the parent-child relationship and it is easily adapted to the teacher-child interaction. The instinctive correctness of this assumption seems to be substantiated by this and other real-life illustrations. Both teachers and parents change their behavior overtime as children mature. If the parent or teacher used only one style (i.e., high task and low relationship) in spite of demonstrated maturity, it is quite probable that the child would remain either dependent or seek independence at the earliest opportunity. The high task/high relationship parent or teacher would produce a dependent child that would fail to mature and become a productive member of society. Even with age, the person remains immature and needs external direction and rewards and may never be able to "stand on his own two feet." Does not the "spoiled brat" emerge from the high relationship and low task parent? Does not a weak and rebellious student come from a low task teacher?

The entire educational system is based on growth development from high structure to little or no structure, from kindergarten to advanced studies in which the structure or task is lessened and the relationship between teacher-leader and student-follower grows systematically less until the term for attending one of the acknowledged high seats of learning in the world, Oxford or Cambridge Universities, is described as "reading for degree or reading for examination." This implies external tasking and requires self-actualization on the part of the student with little, but valued, input from a tutor.

The key to effective classroom leadership becomes the determination of group maturity. Pfeiffer and Jones, (1974) showed group development moving from Immaturity to Maturity through four basic and distinct stages: Why we're here, Bid for Power, Constructive and Esprit de Corps. Another description of these stages was described as: Dependent, Counter Dependent, Independent and Interdependent.

It was further suggested that there were key signals that clue the movement of the group from one stage to the next, i.e., groups move into the "Why we're here!" Form, Stage 1, when those present use the interrogatives: who, what, when, where, how much, etc. Movement from "Storm/Counter Dependent," Stage 2, to Constructive Norm/ Independent, Stage 3, depends on the ability to listen. Someone starts to listen. The greatest prevention to group development from Stage 2 to Stage 3 is usually a strong competitive member or clique (Pfeiffer and Jones, 1974).

Movement from Stage 3 to Stage 4 Esprit-de-corps and interdependent, requires unanimous agreement and full cooperation between teacher and student. Individuals will develop through these stages only as far as they are willing to grow because each step requires that they personally giving up something in order to gain the knowledge required for advancement. For instance, a move from Stage 1 to Stage 2 requires individuals to put aside discussion of the teacher's reasons and objectives and develop their own understand as to the value of the material and it future usability. In fact, a teacher who manages to be in the right place on the task/ relationship continuum may be perceived by students as being High task/High relationship even though they are in reality behaving in terms of low task/low relationship and the students are growing and developing independently. This is the structure that makes for excellent classroom dynamics and learner achievement.

Categories of Learning

Learning takes place in more than one category. A group of educational psychologists from tertiary education, led by Benjamin Bloom in 1956, identified three categories of influence in educational activities sometimes known as **K.S.A.** (Knowledge, Skills, and Attitude).

Knowledge – the cognitive or mental skills.
Skills – body movement triggered by mental activity.
Attitude – growth in feelings or emotional areas.

During the 1990's some cognitive psychologists, lead by Lorin Anderson updated Bloom's taxonomy to reflect a more current word use. Teachers should note the change from nouns to verbs to describe some levels of the familiar Bloom's Taxonomy. This classification of learning behaviors may be considered the objectives of the teaching/learning process. Following a period study or class-based instruction, a student should have acquired new knowledge, skills, and/ or attitudes. Knowledge is gained by using facts, information and data to answer a question or solve a problem. Skills are developing ability, talent, and proficiency in certain physical activities. Attitude is best defined as "a predisposition to act" in a given manner when certain stimuli are present or certain events occur.

Elaboration of the Cognitive and Affective Areas

Academics also produced an elaborate compilation for the cognitive and affective areas, but none in the skills area. This omission was probably due to the work of Simpson in 1972 that included physical movement, coordination, and the motor-skill areas.

The new compilations are divided into three areas (cognitive, affective, and psychomotor) and into categories based on the simplest to the most complex behaviors. The classifications are not complete and other categories have been added; however, Bloom's taxonomy is the most widely known and deals with the cognitive and mental area.

Bloom's Old Version

1. **Knowledge:** arrange, define, duplicate, label, list, memorize, name, order, recognize, relate, recall, repeat, reproduce, state.
2. **Comprehension:** classify, describe, discuss, explain, express, identify, indicate, locate, recognize, report, restate, review, select, translate,
3. **Application:** apply, choose, demonstrate, dramatize, employ, illustrate, interpret, operate, practice, schedule, sketch, solve, use, write.
4. **Analysis:** analyze, appraise, calculate, categorize, compare, contrast, criticize, differentiate, discriminate, distinguish, examine, experiment, question, test.
5. **Synthesis:** arrange, assemble, collect, compose, construct, create, design, develop, formulate, manage, organize, plan, prepare, propose, set up, write.
6. **Evaluation:** appraise, argue, assess, attach, choose compare, defend estimate, judge, predict, rate, core, select, support, value, evaluate

.

New Revised Version

1. **Remembering:** can the student recall or remember the information? [define, duplicate, list, memorize, recall, repeat, reproduce state]
2. **Understanding:** can the student explain ideas or concepts? [classify, describe, discuss, explain, identify, locate, recognize, report, select, translate, paraphrase]
3. **Applying:** can the student use the information in a new way? [choose, demonstrate, dramatize, employ, illustrate, interpret, operate, schedule, sketch, solve, use, write]
4. **Analyzing:** can the student distinguish between the different parts? [appraise, compare, contrast, criticize, differentiate, discriminate, distinguish, examine, experiment, question, test]

5. **Evaluating**: can the student justify a stand or decision? [appraise, argue, defend, judge, select, support, value, evaluate]

6. **Creating:** can the student create new product or point of view? [assemble, construct, create, design, develop, formulate, write]

Bloom's Old Version (1950's)   New Version (1990's)

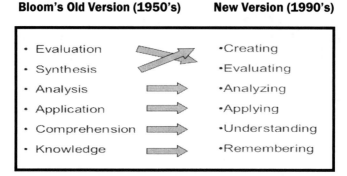

Bloom's Old Version (1950's)	New Version (1990's)
• Evaluation	•Creating
• Synthesis	•Evaluating
• Analysis	•Analyzing
• Application	•Applying
• Comprehension	•Understanding
• Knowledge	•Remembering

Figure 6.4 – Bloom's Taxonomy

The Affective Arena

The development of the affective arena (included the manner of dealing with things emotionally, such as feelings, values, appreciation, enthusiasms, motivations, and attitudes. The five major categories are listed from the simplest behavior to the most complex: (Krathwohl, Bloom, Masia, 1973)

Receiving Phenomena: Awareness, willingness to hear, selected attention. [asks, chooses, describes, follows, gives, holds, identifies, locates, names, points to, selects, sits, erects, replies, uses.]

Responding to Phenomena: Active participation on the part of the learners. Attends and reacts to a particular phenomenon. Learning outcomes may emphasize compliance in responding, willingness to respond, or satisfaction in responding (motivation). [answers, assists, aids, complies, conforms, discusses, greets, helps, labels, performs, practices, presents, reads, recites, reports, selects, tells, writes.]

Valuing: The worth or value a person attaches to a particular object, phenomenon, or behavior. This ranges from simple acceptance to the more complex state of commitment. Valuing is based on the internalization of a set of specified values while clues to these values are expressed in the learner's overt behavior and are often identifiable. [completes, demonstrates, differentiates, explains, follows, forms, initiates, invites, joins, justifies, proposes, reads, reports, selects, shares, studies, works].

Organization: Organizes values into priorities by contrasting different values, resolving conflicts between them, and creating a unique value system.   The emphasis is on comparing, relating, and synthesizing values.   [adheres, alters, arranges, combines, compares, completes, defends, explains, formulates, generalizes, identifies, integrates, modifies, orders, organizes, prepares, relates, synthesizes.]

Internalizing values (characterization): Has a value system that controls their behavior. The behavior is pervasive, consistent, predictable, and most importantly, characteristic of the learner/
Instructional objectives are concerned with the student's general patterns of adjustment (personal, social, emotional). [acts, discriminates, displays, influences, listens, modifies, performs, practices, proposes, qualifies, questions, revises, serves, solves, verifies.]

Psychomotor Skills

The development of psychomotor skills requires practice and is measured in terms of speed, precision, distance, procedures, or techniques in execution. These constructs should be factored into curriculum development and teaching/learning strategies. The seven major categories are listed from the simplest behavior to the most complex (Simpson, 1972).

Perception: The ability to use sensory cues to guide motor activity.   This ranges from sensory stimulation, through cue selection, to translation. [chooses, describes, detects, differentiates, distinguishes, identifies, isolates, relates, selects.]

Set: Readiness to act. It includes mental, physical, and emotional sets. These three sets are dispositions that predetermine a person's response to different situations (sometimes called mindsets). [begins, displays, explains, moves, proceeds, reacts, shows, states, volunteers.]

Guided Response: The early stage in learning a complex skill that includes imitation and trial and error. Adequacy of performance is achieved by practicing. [copies, traces, follows, react, reproduce, responds.]

Mechanism: This is the intermediate stage in learning a complex skill. Learned responses have become habitual and the movements can be performed with some confidence and proficiency. [assembles, calibrates, constructs, dismantles, displays, fastens, fixes, grinds, heats, manipulates, measures, mends, mixes, organizes, sketches.]

Complex Overt Response: The skillful performance of motor acts that involve complex movement patterns. Proficiency is indicated by a quick, accurate, and highly coordinated performance, requiring a minimum of energy. This category includes performing without hesitation, and automatic performance. For example, players often utter sounds of satisfaction or expletives as soon as they hit a tennis ball or throw a football because they can tell by the feel of the act what the result will produce. The key words are the same as Mechanism, but uses adverbs or adjectives to indicate that performance is quicker, better, more accurate. [assembles, builds, calibrates, constructs, dismantles, displays, fastens, fixes, grinds, heats, manipulates, measures, mends, mixes, organizes, sketches.]

Adaptation: Skills are well developed and the individual can modify movement patterns to fit special requirements. [adapts, alters, changes, rearranges, reorganizes, revises, varies.]

Origination: Creating new movement patterns to fit a particular situation or specific problem. Learning outcomes emphasize creativity based upon highly developed skills. [arranges, builds, combines, composes, constructs, creates, designs, initiate, makes, originates.]

A general view of the operational dynamics of a classroom reveal both organized effort and goal directed human behavior that increases intellectual capacity and creates an atmosphere conducive to learning.

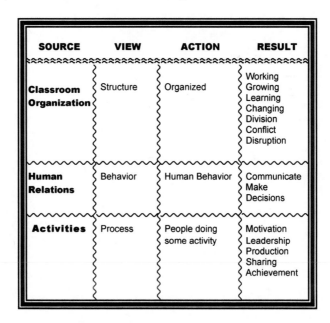

SOURCE	VIEW	ACTION	RESULT
Classroom Organization	Structure	Organized	Working Growing Learning Changing Division Conflict Disruption
Human Relations	Behavior	Human Behavior	Communicate Make Decisions
Activities	Process	People doing some activity	Motivation Leadership Production Sharing Achievement

Figure 6.5 - Framework for viewing classroom operations.

CHAPTER SEVEN

Sympathetic Inputs and Cybernetics

Theoretical and Applied Analysis

Theoretical and applied analysis of the teaching/learning process provides an understanding of the deeper constructs of behavior required to be a transformational leader in education. The conflict between supervision and transformational leadership may be overcome through a consciousness of the interconnectedness of all aspects of education. At times, new words are needed to shake off the lethargy of the past and become a dynamic and functioning force in education.

Notwithstanding contemporary concepts, the constructs that inform the transformational view of leadership in education are rooted in the distant past. The pristine words; such as, sympathetic and cybernetics have positive value and meaning for education. Improvement is required to provide a transformational perspective relevant to the current needs of education. A look at these key words is required to fully understand the function of supervision and leadership in education. Cybernetics deals with a feedback system that must be understood by those who would either guide or supervise in the field of education. The other word "sympathetic" added to the present mix can move responsible educators into the affective domain where one can feel the same thing that others are feeling. This sense of sameness and the ability to share the common feelings that provide affinity between persons is a necessary ingredient to transformational leadership in education.   The affective domain permits action based on feeling with others, rather than viewing the situation from the top of the Ivy tower. The science of cybernetics and the construct of a sympathetic system combine to provide leadership with a guiding framework to influence the actions and attitudes that produce dramatic change in individuals and groups in various aspects of education by action based on a mutual understanding of existing conditions in both the system and the classroom.

Essential Elements

Sympathetic inputs and cybernetics can assist leaders in a clear understanding of how individuals and organizations mature and progress. Sympathetic inputs include understanding, concern, compassion, sensitivity, and a supportive attitude. Much as the autonomic nervous system of the human body, these impulses must be controlled by automatic responses and be constant to be effective. This behavior must be action or response that occurs without the conscious control of the teacher. Cybernetic controls are replications of the natural system or preplanned responses to certain situations or stimuli. The thermostat is an example of a programmed response. Also, the teacher must understand that there are automatic processes occurring in the students as well.

Teachers often considers a principled and practical operation sufficient to guarantee growth and progress. This attitude often obstructs the inherent factors of growth and causes both individuals and the institution to be content with mediocrity. A willingness to settle for something less than the best causes everyone to suffer from a predictable disease and to become strangulated in vital areas of growth and progress. The willingness to settle for mediocre operations also brings about a lack of global perspective and produces neglect in the areas of instruction and guidance in a learning environment.

Understanding how individuals and groups develop and grow is a multifaceted process. It is difficult to explain how the human brain works, how the inner workings of a computer function, or how people behave in groups. The field of cybernetics deals with the science of complex electronic calculating machines and the human nervous system in an attempt to explain the nature of the brain.   The term "cybernetics" comes from the Greek, *kybernetes*, meaning "helmsman." Most leaders are so far removed from the seafaring age that even the concept of "helmsman" escapes the vocabulary. A "helmsman" was the "the person at the helm; the one who steers the ship." The "helm" is defined as "the complete steering gear, including the wheel or tiller, rudder, etc." In addition, the helmsman must know the nature of the ship, the capacity of the crew, the nature of the currents, the strength of the winds, and the nature of the waters in which the ship is moving. Making the translation and/or application to leadership is not difficult. To steer is to direct the course or progress of someone or something. To supervise an educational system or instruct a group of students, one must have similar knowledge of human behavior and the educational environment just as a helmsman had to understand the ship, the crew and the conditions under which the ship sailed in the present environment.

A Cybernetic Process—the Thermostat

A modern construct that demonstrates the cybernetic process is the thermostat. A thermostat is designed to sense changes in the environment and activate controls that can make adjustments to the surroundings.   This is akin to the function of a teacher in the classroom or a supervisor in the school office. Familiarity with this instrument on the wall may assist educators in understanding how the system and the environment of education changes, how the people function in a changing society, and the leader's role in changing the conditions or atmosphere where they serve. Study diagram below. It is a strong instructor for leadership.

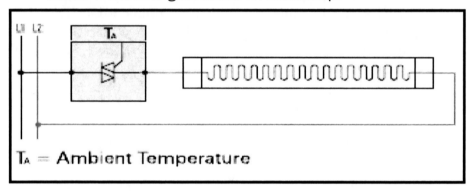

Figure 7.1 - Input – Process – Output - Feedback Model

Early in my professional life there were two plaques on my desk: "Faith without works is dead!" and "Ideas are funny little things, they don't work unless you do!" Both plaques spoke of "work." Also, it was understood that the old saying "Prayer changes things" did not provide the whole proposition. People received the wrong idea from a fragment of an adage. Many assumed they could simply say a few word in a religious environment and do nothing themselves, and some divine power would step in and fix the problems. However, prayer is similar to an idea: it does not work without personal attention and action. The third plague dealt with "people." If the interpretation of all the plaques were understood they reminded me that to accomplish anything or to make any achievements one had to "work" with "people." Also, it reminded me that God was not going to do my work.

The actual construct of the proverb was "Prayer changes

people and people change things." The same is true in the teaching/learning process. Teachers must pay attention to the student and remember that where there is no evidence of learning, there has been no teaching. Learning is a personal discovery process, the superior knowledge and experience of the teacher does not guarantee a student will learn. It is the student that must understand and learn. Therefore, those who administer education should remember the obvious variation of "minister" and "administer."

The construct of "minister" relates to serving the needs of an individual; while the word "administer" suggests a broader meaning of supervising the actions of others.   An awareness of both serving the needs of the individual and caring for the larger needs of the institution come together in the concept of sympathetic leadership cybernetics. Poor or weak teachers should be removed from the classroom and if the "Peter principle" is followed, these ineffective teachers may be advanced to supervisory positions. Could this be a reason for the poor oversight that exists in most educational systems?

Teaching is the Ability to Influence Others

Some assume that placing a person in a given position will change things; however, individuals must be changed before a group can change. To utilize personal influence from a positional role; such as, principal or teacher, personal action must be tuned to the affective domain and all action based on that understanding. The chief requirement of educational leadership is the ability to influence others to follow one voluntarily toward stated goals. Thus, one can clearly see the fallacy in using only positional power without the sympathetic cybernetic function that leads to personal and direct influence.

Authentic leadership will use all four of the essential leadership elements: vision, courage, integrity, and perseverance.   A prerequisite element must be added: knowledge of how individuals develop and learn. Unless one in a leadership role understands the individual dynamics of learning, utilizing the other essential aspects will be futile. A precondition to utilizing vision, courage, integrity, and perseverance is the basic knowledge of how individuals learn, mature and grow intellectually and emotionally.

Classroom Cybernetics

Classroom cybernetics simply speaks to the control factor instructors have over the environment. Cybernetics in education purports that the teacher understands the environment and the individuals and has the ability to guide or steer individuals and the class through ups and downs of class time with a clear vision.

Vision.   Teachers must have a strategic vision of the future needs of each student and the class as a whole and the ability to develop and follow an agenda to reach the stated goals. A dream has no agenda; a goal has a vision with a clear agenda, and a feasible plan that deals with the realities of getting from the existent to the next level of achievement or advancement. This vision must be articulated with a certain courage and boldness, that some may call daring and a challenge to current assumptions. Such boldness suggests an audacity not normally found outside transformational leadership.

Courage.   A classroom instructor or a tutor must possess a confident courage and fluency of speech that enables a clear articulation of a visualization that would alter the existing state of affairs. There is no substitute for courage. Individual courage does not mean that one acts or behaves without a measure of respect for the conditions that currently exist; rather it is the ability to function in spite of feelings of anxiety and apprehension caused by anticipated dangers. Fearlessness without integrity creates a less than honorable situation. Respect for classroom teachers simply means that all concerned closely observes pays attention to the current situation.

Integrity. A certain reliability and veracity is required to be a learning leader and convince others to follow one toward stated goals. A good teacher speaks the truth and maintains an obvious sincerity without artificiality. This gives authenticity to the class environment and breeds trust and loyalty which convince learners to look at and pay attention to all aspects of a teacher's conduct and demeanor.

Perseverance. There must be a sense of urgency demonstrated in both tone and action about the specifics of the learning journey in the classroom. Difficulties must not dissuade an attitude of firmness about the stated goals or the plan of action and a determined resolve to progress toward individual and class intellectual achievements. Such resolve is required to secure the attention and follow-ship of students who will in turn facilitate the teaching/learning process. Perseverance can assure a firm insistence on the vital steps in the plan of action as long as the S-curve of growth is noticeably understood and appreciated.

S-curve of Growth

An understanding of the S-curve of growth, that all living organisms and organizations exhibit is essential to comprehending the inner workings of a classroom. The S-curve of growth has three phases: a period called the lag phase (I) when preparation is being made for learning and stimulates interest in the subject at hand. The period of acute interest and excited inquiry is a time of actual learning called the exponential or logarithmic phase (II). This period of learner involvement will normally climax in self-activity and independent learning where the student and/or class develop a healthy academic environment through constructive coordination of differing facets. At this point in intellectual development, a stationary phase (III) usually develops because of satisfaction of learning and the lack of awareness of the long-term need for the information. When this crisis in the teaching/learning process is not met, the energies and resources normally used for learning are re-channeled into personal interests to maintain a *status quo*; thus, the leveling off period is entered when learning slows and the knowledge base stabilizes. This critical stationary phase may develop into a learning plateau unless the student and the class receive intellectual stimulation from a learning leader. Sometimes the standard approach to classroom development and dynamic learning is frustrating and the automatic nature of intellectual excitement fails to mature. The nature of instruction and structure move into a transformational mode at the point to assure further learning.

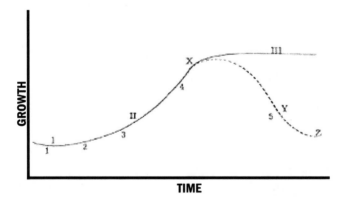

Figure 7.2 – Diagram of the normal growth curve of classroom learning: I-lag phase, II-logarithmic phase, III-stationary phase, X-point of crisis. Y-decreased interest. Z-fixed attitude that hinders development.. Numbers 1-5 are the same in Figure 7.3.

Provided the organization survives, more formal rules are increasingly imposed on the organizational constituency. This process produces a vicious cycle that impairs the effectiveness of the organization. The sociologists claim that if the organization survives the early developing years, the constituency numbers normally increase and the property becomes more aesthetic. There are at least five anticipated states in this development that leadership must understand.

Stages of Classroom Development

The normal stages of classroom development are: (1) an early weak association with the teacher and classmates, (2) an acceptable relationship structure is established, (3) a time of maximum efficiency in learning and intellectual stimulation occurs, (4) a more formal arrangements where strong and weak students become evident, and (5) without patient perseverance on the part of the learning leader, the learning environment may become stale and students loose interest in the subject. This demoralization may be avoided if, at crisis point (A) which may come early in a class period, the learning leader brings creative initiative in the classroom environment and the essential elements of the subject at hand are clearly articulated, acceptable learning levels may continue. The objective is to restore continuation of the learning curve (A-B).

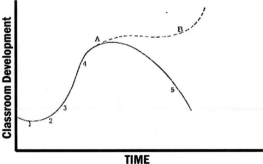

Figure 7.3 – Five stages of classroom learning

The essential classroom dynamics to assure learning and academic development are: sufficient mental nutrients to feed and stimulate the brain, activities that provide outlets for energy in useful forms, sufficient time to master the material, adequate classroom space and environment that is conducive to learning, and the intellectual viability of individual students functioning at an acceptable level. Translating these facts into the present learning environment is the real task of the teacher. Understanding the thermostat on the wall could facilitate a grasp of the cybernetic process by which an instructor knows when the classroom environment is right for the next step.

Consider how the thermostat is perceived. When workers continued to adjust the thermostat up and down they were asked to explain how the instrument worked. One answer, "On whatever temperature you set the thermostat, that's the temperature the air comes out." The answer was dazzling and demonstrated a total lack of understanding of the thermostat function. My mother-in-law has an example of a different view. She thinks through the thermostat she can "hot shot" the heat and air conditioning system. If the house is cold, she turns the temperature setting high and says, "I hot shot it; it will get warm in a minute." She actually believes the furnace gets hot quicker the higher one sets the thermostat. The converse is true for her, the air conditioner works faster if one lowers the temperature setting to the lowest setting. So much for conventional wisdom or the wisdom of the uninformed as it relates to the teaching/learning process. Yet, some in the field of education seem to function in a similar manner.

Leaders in education must be adequately informed about the science of cybernetics. Understanding the thermostat could be a benefit to both leader and people. At least it would show an understanding for the lag time that is required to bring about change in individuals and in institutions. Teachers and students do not perform just because someone expects them to make high marks. No matter how much one attempts to "hot shot" the system, it will move at the normal pace of social change. To push the envelope is to provoke conflict.

Educators should not attempt to manipulate the system. It is as foolish as one attempting to "hot shot" a thermostat. Teachers and supervisors should exercise patience and work toward motivation rather than manipulation. It takes a little longer but works with the system. Those who do not understand these dynamics of a cybernetic system may not last long or well serve the field of education. The thermostat is a cybernetic system by understand the function and operation one can more clearly grasp the construct of sympathetic cybernetics based on the Input-Process-Output-Feedback System below:

1. **Input** – the operator transmits desired setting;
2. **Process** – the system determines how the HEAT/AC should operate;
3. **Output** – the cybernetic system of the thermostat measures the ambient temperature and sends a signal to the HEAT/AC system;
4. **Feedback** – the temperature is measured and the system operates according to the pre-set level;
5. **Adjustment or Confirmation** – after the feedback is analyzed the pre-set can be re-set to a different level by the operator or remain the same.

Application of the Cybernetic System to Education

1. **Input** could clearly be seen as the function of the teacher and the textbook or syllabus;
2. **Process** is the communication necessary in the teaching/learning process;
3. **Output** is the actual performance of the student;
4. **Feedback** is a positive or negative assessment of student performance through exams and essays on which the teacher makes a decision for correction or confirmation;
5. **Adjustment or Confirmation** – Negative feedback requires an adjustment or correction to either the curriculum or the instruction or both.

6. Confirmation – Positive feedback deserves commendation or confirmation of a job well done and should be done publicly through grade reports and teaching awards.

A Sympathetic System

A sympathetic system is sophisticated and appears to be complicated whether it is the human autonomic nervous system or the automatic workings inside a computer; however, when one understands how a system works it appears entirely different. These systems although complex are not complicated when one comprehends the inner workings. Knowing how the system works makes the difference. When one works with the system, a **synergy** or "working together" develops that simplifies the process. For example, when one combines word processing skills with the inner workings of a PC, a real synergy occurs. The sympathetic cybernetic approach to the classroom can remove much of the complication and enable teachers to appear more sophisticated in approaching issues related to the teaching/learning process. Synergy occurs when two or more forces work, so the combined effort is greater than the sum of the individual efforts. Synergy requires an understanding of how the system actually works. Understanding requires both discernment and comprehension that permits a reconciliation of differences; thus, it becomes sympathetic. This is what leadership is all about: the ability to influence both individuals and circumstances based on a sameness of feeling. In fact, individuals are influenced to change and in turn these changed individuals make the necessary changes in the learning environment.

W.A.S.P –Weakness and Strengths Plan

WASP is an assessment strategy used to analyze weaknesses and strengths in any situation involving individuals. It is similar to asset and liabilities in a business balance sheet and similar to determining driving and restraining forces. In the teaching/learning process, it becomes necessary to look at both teacher and student identifying the internal and external factors that are favorable and unfavorable in relation to performing their task. Factors to consider are: background, previous education, home and family environment, health, appearance, social skills, learning capacity and general attitude. Knowing this information and understanding the impact it may have on the teaching/learning process is of great value to the classroom dynamics.

CHAPTER EIGHT

Affective Direction and Education

The Affective Domain

A basic assumption in education is that student behavior and achievement are governed by affective well-being. Understanding the affective domain provides useful information for those who guide students in personal growth and academic development. To improve the knowledge of the affective domain in education a planning and teaching model with general application is needed. A scheme for classifying and organizing instructional material must be established that will chart the scope and sequence of instruction. An instructional design based on developmental theory could provide the tools and a sense of direction that make it possible for teachers to prepare and implement instructional goals.

Teaching goals should enable students to recognize and understand that emotions, attitudes, values, surroundings and associations with others influence what they learn. The teaching goals should make students aware of the outcomes and consequences that may result from feelings of joy, anger, fear, surprise, or distress. Teachers need to instruct students to weigh the outcome of decisions with reference to their effect on them and others and recognize different ways they could respond. Finally, students must understand the nature, forms, and consequences of aggression and apply their knowledge of emotions, attitudes, and values toward positive, real-life experience.

An effective curriculum and teaching model will assist students with self-concept, interpersonal relationships, and their feelings about the educational environment. This aesthetic sensitivity determines, to a large extent, the degree of motivation the student has to achieve an educational objective. Proceeding from the known and accepted, a synthesis of models may be used in plotting a course which leads to planning and teaching in both the cognitive and affective domains. This means that both the thinking and feeling of students are the responsibility of the teacher.

Teacher Implementation of Cognitive and Affective Behaviors

In breaking away from a strict cognitive emphasis, teachers must understand possibility of developing both the thinking and feeling processes in association with the learning of content. This process clearly portrays the three dimensions of teaching and learning that should be incorporated into a Model for Implementing Cognitive and Affective Behaviors. It is important that these dimensions be understood: (1) **Curriculum** – traditional subject matter content, (2) **Teacher behavior** –ways of teaching, and (3) **Learner behavior** – ways of thinking and feeling Having established a three dimensional framework for model building, it becomes necessary to establish plans for both cognitive and affective development. Originally written as a scheme to classify levels of mental operations, Taxonomy has proven to be a valuable working tool for lesson planners and curriculum builders. The taxonomical classification of education goals provides for an upward progression from "the recall of information" to "making judgments." The progression is from the simple to the complex in reverse order.

Operational Definitions of Cognitive Goals

The cognitive goals that appear in the left hand column are in summary form. The operational definitions in the right hand column suggest behavior related to each goal. The goals and operational definitions are in ascending order 1 to 6.

Cognitive Goals:

Operational Definitions:

6. Evaluation – Judgment in terms of internal and external criteria.

>**6**. The child decides, a judgment of right and wrong, good or bad is based on established criteria.

5. Synthesis – Production of a unique communication, plan or set of operations

>**5**. The child creates a product or designs a unique plan.

4. Analysis -- Breakdown of communication into elements, relationships, organization.

>**4**. The child reasons and determines parts, order, and relationships.

3. Application – Use abstractions in particular and concrete situations.

>**3**. The child applies information and uses it to solve problems.

2. Comprehension – Lowest level of understanding; information is translated and interpreted

>**2**. The child explains and demonstrates his/her understanding.

1. Knowledge – Involves the recall of specifics, terms, facts, and methods.

>**1**. The child knows.

igure 8.1 – Cognitive goals and definitions.

The Cognitive Taxonomy is of value to teachers in the following ways: (1) It establishes a learning order and moves from the lower to the higher order thinking processes. (2) It may be used to prepare objectives because it suggests learning outcomes. (3) It provides a target for clarifying desired learner behavior. (4) When appropriate "cueing verbs" are used to direct learner behavior and the outcome is predictable.

Operational Definitions for Affective Goals

The affective goals in the left column are in summary form. The operational descriptions in the right column suggests the disposition, attitude, and feelings of the child associated with each goal. The goals and responses are ascending 1 to 5.

Affective Goals:

Operational Definitions:

5.Characterization>>>>
Internalization of a value.
Value system consistent with
behavior.

5. The child voices belief
and affirms values.

4. Organization >>>>>>
Recognize pervasive values,
determines Inter-relationships
of values, organizes value
systems.

4. The child reviews, questions,
and arranges values into an
ordered system or plan.

3. Valuing >>>>>>>>>>
Accepting, preferring, and
making commitment to a
value.

3. The child chooses a concept
or behavior believed to be
worthy.

2. Responding >>>>>>
Willingness to respond,
motivated, gains satisfaction if
responding

2. The child wants to discuss or
explain.

1. Receiving >>>>>>>>
Pays attention, is aware,
takes information into
account.

1. The child displays
attentiveness; listens, notices,
and observes.

Figure 8.2 – Affective Goals

Theoretical Constructs

Several theoretical constructs about mature learners regardless of age must be considered. These should include the concept of transactional distance, dialogue and support, structure and general and specialized competence, and self-directedness. The whole model must be tied into a theory of learning and based on the perceptions of mature learners.

Learning Theory

Support for the application of Learning Theories come directly from the concepts of Pedagogy, Andragogy and the synergetic learning designs. Kapp, a German scholar, introduced the term to European educators in 1833 to explain the educational theories of Plato. The term "Andragogy" surfaced in the 1920s and was widely used in Europe by the 1960s. The constructs of Andragogy were reintroduced into North and South America by Lindeman (1927) and Knowles (1970) and was defined as the art and science of helping serious students learn.

Andragogy vs. Pedagogy

Knowles (1980) revised Lindeman (1927) and created four assumptions, which formed the basis of a theory of Andragogy in the United States. Knowles assumptions were: (1) as students mature, their self-concept moves from dependency toward self-direction; (2) the accumulated experiences of mature students may be used in learning; (3) The readiness of mature students to learn is closely related to developmental tasks or social roles; and (4) learning becomes more problem-oriented and less subject-oriented as students move forward in time. Knowles defined Andragogy methods in terms of assisting mature learners as distinguished from pedagogy meaning "the art and science" of teaching immature learners. Somehow the concept of pedagogy coming from the Greek meaning "to lead a child" became in modern time to mean "the art and science" of instruction or teaching methods and generally identified the profession. This concept tragically locked teachers into existing methodology that had little relation to the maturity or capacity of the learner. The construct of Andragogy was an effort by Knapp, Lindeman, Knowles, et al to bring the profession into modern times. Teachers and educational systems have moved slowly, sometimes kicking and screaming all the way to the use of computers. the Internet and other interactive mechanisms.

The Process of Andragogy

First, a climate conducive to learning must be established. Then, an educational structure friendly to participative planning should be produced to determine the needs of the learners. Next, objectives to direct the learning process must be formulated. This suggests the need for a plan to design learning activities and the operational implementation of these activities. Finally, the assessment process must include an evaluation of these activities in terms of the needs of the learners and the effectiveness of teachers.

Andragogy should be seen as a set of ideals that may be applied with mature learners. The concept is not universally applicable to all learners (Verduin and Clark 1991). Pratt (1988) suggested that self-directedness may be a situational attribute used to determine the maturity of the learners who would benefit from the constructs of Andragogy. Beder (1985) postulated that the formality or informality of the subject at hand may be a stronger influence on the choice of teaching style than the age of the students. Gorham (1985) found that most teachers who support Andragogy actually make few changes in the pedagogical style when teaching mature learners. Notwithstanding a continuing argument in education over the role of the teacher and the true characteristics of learners, Andragogy, as a theory and philosophy for teaching mature learners, is used to understand the difference between maturity levels of students in terms of self-directedness, experience, developmental readiness, and problem orientation (Knowles 1980).

Synergistic Learning Designs are Useful

Instead of taking an all or nothing view, in varying degrees the teaching in lower grades should be pedagogic and in the higher grades a more andragogic approach that uses synergistic learning designs. Traditional pedagogic methods are used when necessary to instruct, tutor, or communicate specific content essential to the subject at hand. Both the formality of the discipline and learner readiness guide the teaching process. It is understood that developmental tasks for learners vary among individuals and that this variation may occur among chronologically similar students. Although some teachers lack the ability to shift between pedagogical and Andragogy teaching orientations, experienced and mature students learn to adjust to different styles and learning environments. Exposing learners to both teaching styles should produce balanced and adaptive learners. However, one should remember that those who do not adapt will become drop-outs unless special effort is taken to tutor them. Care must be taken not to dumb down the class just to assist the slower ones. Private and individual attention is the best solution. These students should be discretely identified and given special attention without the stigma of being losers. No student should be left behind when time and tutoring are available. When there is no time for extra tutoring, the system must be notified of the special needs of the at risk students.

Process vs. Content

Some methods work better with the young or inexperienced learners while others are more suited for the mature learner. Through the years the system has well defined the pedagogic methods of teaching the young; however, the mechanisms of working with the mature learner and the at risk students are more recent in the literature. Essentially, the newer methods deal with all learners based on their intellectually maturity rather than age, time or grade. The defining of the newer methodology focuses in four areas: (1) self-directedness; (2) previous experience as a resource; (3) learning related to real life problems, and (4) increasing competence for life tasks. Knowles acknowledged that the essence of his model of education was its emphasis on **process** (manner, means, and procedure), whereas, the pedagogical model placed more importance on **content**. It was assumed that mature learners were qualitatively rather than quantitatively different (Knowles 1973, 1984).

Maintaining Momentum of Participation

One basic problem in dealing with individuals in the educational context is that it is difficult to maintain the momentum of participation overtime. This requires extensive dialogue/ support by teachers with a repertoire of sophisticated teaching strategies as well as a grounded philosophy and a comprehensive knowledge of students as learners. A significant fact in the matter is that most students capable of being mature learners have never experienced being treated as a mature learner in he classroom environment and they do not automatically adjust to the process after such an immersion in an opposite modality. Their previous educational experience was different and brings with it a negative conditioning that hampers learning. Consequently, teachers must make the transition obvious and explain the reasons for the change in methods.

CHAPTER NINE

Formal and Informal Learning

Only Blatant Intimidation

Reading sociology in a Northern university many years ago, my afternoon schedule placed me in a class taught by the Chair of the Department. The first day the professor said, "I give seven "F's" each term. If I only had seven students I would flunk them all." My inner voice screamed silently...this is education? My mother was a teacher; her knowledge of Latin taught me that the construct of education came from *educere* [*e* meaning "out" and *ducere* "to lead or bring up"]. This did not sound as if this professor understood that he should take our hand and lead us out of ignorance into the light of knowledge; rather he chose to intimidate and threaten to eliminate all who could not navigate or get past his flawed teaching style. There were no expressed concerns for the students, no nurturing or caring, only blatant intimidation of vulnerable students who were paying tuition to be personally and academically insulted.

The first three Friday exams all the class but two were scoring in the 40's. A bright black lady and the author were scoring in the 60's. No one could find a way to pass his exams. After three weeks it was decided that we would not read the text written by the professor or take notes, but just listen and see if we could plot a course forward. Meeting at lunch, my friend said, "We must read the chapter before class." After a little negotiation it was decided that we would only read the footnotes, under the tables and graphs, and take notice of italic and bold words. With this approach we both scored in the 80's and the rest of the class remained in the 40's. The professor asked us to remain after class and said, "You have discovered my secret and if you share it, you will be in the seven who fail this course."

Was that real Ivy League education or an abuse of the basics of teaching? One of the fundamental requirements of teaching may be "excite and direct the self-activity of the student and as a rule tell them nothing they can learn for themselves," but this teacher's approach was naïve and arrogant. Writing a textbook and placing important data in the footnotes, graphs, and operational terms in italic or bold type may create a worthy text, but it does not guarantee good classroom instruction. When the "secrets" of the teacher are kept from the student, it becomes a distortion of instruction and a debased version of education. Then to fail those who could not read the map without a legend or key to understand the symbols used becomes a travesty. This is not what education is about.

The first half "excite and direct the self-activity" was totally ignored, plus the threat of failure was a violation of an established tenet of philosophy: "One can never reach a positive conclusion beginning with a negative premise." The teaching/learning process is a two-way street. Students must be taken by the hand and led forward as the teacher shines a guiding light on the pathway toward knowledge. It is a synergistic process. Teachers and administrators who may rise to a level of incompetence (if they remain in education) should have the personal integrity to stay out of the classroom. Students and learning are the reasons for the existence of schools; not to provide secure employment for those without genuine interest and commitment to the teaching/learning process.

Structure as a Function of Learning

Dialogue, structure, and learner autonomy are foundational elements in understanding education. Dialogue should be seen as support for the learner. It must not be only a way to get answers concerning methodology or content, but should be seen as emotional support for the learner. A high dialogue methodology is essential to attract and retain adult students.

Structure as a function of the formality of the subject matter suggests the need for specialized competence in a field. This is a situational attribute (Pratt 1988) based largely on the learner's personal knowledge and expertise. Faculty must consider the learner's situational attribute in the area of specialized competence when dealing with an educational transaction and in structuring a learning situation. Dialogue becomes a means of determining specialized competence and a guide adjusting structure to meet the needs of the learner.

In Figure 9.1, the large items suggest formal learning based on the curriculum and instructions received. The small items denote the informal learners who learn perhaps in spite of the quality of instructions, but because of personal interest and motivation. Such learners are self-starters and independent thinkers who can take a little of what the teacher says and learn a lot from personally engaging the material and applying intellectual competence and maturity to the subject at hand based on the foundation of their knowledge base.

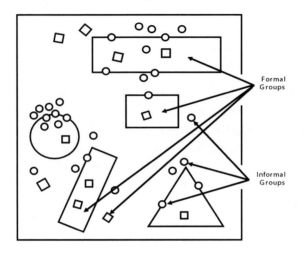

Figure 9.1 Formal and Informal Learning

General and Specialized Competence

General competence defined as self-directedness by Verduin and Clark (1991) is not adequate to determine specialized competence. Skill in discussion, verbal discourse, or the ability to write well is not sufficient evidence of competence. The learner must be able to read and deal with additive and variant material, differentiate important and unimportant data, and record the meaning of important data in an abbreviated form. The ability to write well is a vital skill in faculty/student dialogue, but alone does not signify specialized competency necessary to complete graduate study.

Advanced studies require both general and specialized competency in the field. A highly-structured field such as mathematics requires more specialized competency on the part of the learner than a low-structured field such as education. Overview or entry-level courses require the least specialized competence. Graduate level interdisciplinary courses may not require a great deal of specialized competency but does require considerable amounts of general competency.

Teachers in education programs tend to generalize the nature of learning. This is done on the basis of Andragogy and other general philosophies that relate to mature learners. Theory focuses on learning in the ideal world. Learning takes place in the real world of family and community, politics and government. All these must be factored into the structure of the teaching/learning transaction together with learner autonomy, dialogue/support, structure, self-directedness, and general and specialized competence. The formal nature of the teaching process must join the informal character of the learning process if the classroom dynamics are to be productive.

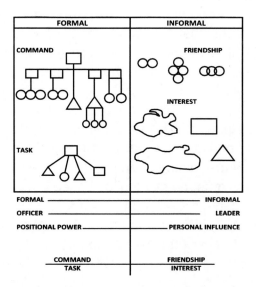

Figure 9.2 – Formal and Informal Classroom Structure

Plowing Around the Stumps

There are three reasons for planning in education. First, educational leadership must (1) plan for the future. Unless this is done one cannot fulfill the second reason for planning which is to (2) take advantage of opportunities. When leadership understands the purpose, knows the objectives, values the goals, and is clear on the standards by which achievement will be measured, they can take advantage of each opportunity to advance the purpose. Only then should leadership take time to (3) deal with problems. Many problems are solved through using the opportunities that circumstance presents. Usually this is accomplished by asking three questions: What can be done better? What can be done differently? What can be done new? In other words, transformational leaders know how to "plow around the stumps!"

What is meant by "plowing around the stumps?" An example would be a family traveling west in the pioneer days of the United States. After many days of weary travel a hilltop is spotted with a good view of a well watered valley. Once a decision is made that this would be a good place to raise a family, the first priority is to look to the future. Winter is coming and a cabin must be built, a garden planted, and food stores laid up to survive the anticipated winter. Then the ability to observe opportunities takes over: cutting the trees would clear the land for a cabin, produce logs for the construction, provide firewood for the winter, and open the ground for a sun-drenched garden. Now, the major problem of tree stumps must be overlooked based on the first priority of building a cabin and planting a garden. One can imagine the wife saying, "John you need to move that stump it will block the front door of the cabin!" John's intelligent response would be, "If I take time to deal with that problem, there will be no cabin, no garden and no food stores for the winter." John constructs a cabin, gathers fire wood, plants the garden by plowing around the stumps and goes hunting for meat for the winter. With a warm cabin and food for the winter, John can think about the future solution to the "problem."

After a couple of winters and the discomfort of walking around the stump at the front door, a log-chain is placed around the rotting stump and attached to the plow-horse. The old problem stump is easily pulled out of the way. Dealing with the future and taking advantages of opportunities can take care of many problems. This is a lesson that transformational leaders must learn quickly or surely fail. To become preoccupies with problem solving is to trample a previously mentioned rule of philosophy: one can never reach a positive conclusion beginning with a negative premise. Another rule expands this idea: a positive implies a negative. When the positive points are clearly stated, the problem is partially solved. One needs only to add a little creative wisdom to the process to complete the solution.

Planning Process determines Action

In order to achieve motility there must be purposeful action not just activity or busyness, there must be a planning process. When educational leadership is sure of where they are going and clear of what they are attempting to do, the best methods can be used to complete the process. When this is done adequately in a timely manner the process will achieve satisfactory results. This can only be done if the choice of teaching/learning mechanisms is a result of a planning process.

Purpose, Objectives, Goals, and Standards

The **purpose** is singular and directional. It provides a general direction toward the long-range outcomes of the subject at hand. Although singular, this purpose must be sub-divided into reachable and measurable objectives and goals. **Objectives, goals, and standards** are always plural, similar to parallel structure in sentence structure. Some may choose to use goals, objectives, aims, etc., but the rule follows: each must be a subset of the previous order. A purpose may be divided into two or more objectives. An objective is divided into two or more goals. If only one objective were determined, it would be a restatement of the purpose. Standards are criteria by which achievements are measured and must be multiple.

This follows the same rule as an outline in writing: one cannot have a "1" without a "2" or an "A" without a "B", etc.

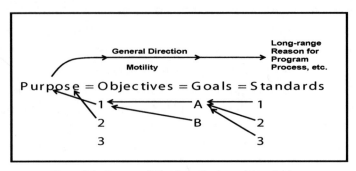

Figure 9.3-- Purpose, Objectives, Goals, and Standards

An **objective** is a specific aspect of the purpose; when accomplished, it advances the intention in the right direction. **Goals** are specific aspects of an objective; when reached, an objective is accomplished and the purpose is advanced. A standard is a measurement by which accomplishments or performance can be assessed. Normally, there are three categories of **standards**: (1) performance, (2) efficiency, and (3) effectiveness. **Performance** is the ability to carry out, accomplish, function, and discharge a duty or deed. **Efficiency** is productivity without loss or waste. When **effectiveness** is assessed, it demonstrates readiness for advancement or action and suggests adequacy or competency to proceed.

When educational leadership deals with the purpose explicit in the curriculum, direction is provided that guides instruction and action. Normally one is given direction only once, but may constantly need guidance along any journey. Consequently, a classroom instructor must be guided by the curriculum for the subject at hand. The general capacity of students to determine performance at specific competency levels is measured by the efficiency of reaching objectives and goals. The goals are milestones along the journey to measure progress and to provide encouragement. Should goals be divided into short-ranged and long-ranged goals? The long-ranged goals exist to prevent discouragement with short-ranged failures. There will be failures because all human endeavors consist of human beings with limitations. However, the setting of priorities improves efficiency and effectiveness in the teaching/learning process.

Gregory's Laws of Teaching

John Milton Gregory (1822-1998) gave up the study of law (1884) to become a Baptist minister and then became a teacher and administrator in higher education, working primarily in Michigan and Illinois. He held important educational positions during his long life. . Gregory was head of the classical school in Detroit, State Superintendent of Public Instruction in Michigan, President of Kalamazoo College, and the organizer and founding President of the University of Illinois. Gregory advocated the integration of a classically-based liberal arts curriculum with the existing industrial and agricultural studies. He clearly articulated his understanding of teaching in his book, The Seven Laws of Teaching (1884). These profound and timeless declarations governing the art of teaching are available to a new generation of educators. Those who understand and follow these basic constructs will receive the praise of grateful students in a positive learning environment. Gregory's timeless insights have universal application. One who understands and follows this basic set of laws will receive the praise of grateful students in a positive learning environment.

Gregory's Laws remain relevant to the needs of learners. They are presented here in the simplest form:

1. Teachers must know the subject they would teach.
2. Learners must listen with interest to the material being taught.
3. The language, used in teaching must be common to both teacher and learner.
4. The facts to be taught must be learned through facts already known.

5. The teacher must excite and direct the self-activity of the student, and as a rule tell them nothing they can learn on their own.
6. The learners must reproduce in their own words the facts to be learned. Memorization is the first level of learning. After the facts of the lesson are clear there is an elementary degree of understanding. The next step in the process is the ability to paraphrase a thought or concept in one's own words. Finally, the learners must search for evidence to support their understanding and make an effort to apply what was learned. Application is required to reinforce the learning process.
7. At least one-third of teaching/study/class time should be given to review and/or application of the lessons learned.

Neglect these fundamentals and one's teaching credentials and even subject-specific certification will be useless pieces of paper. Those who attempt to teach without Gregory's perspective will become frustrated and produce a class of passive and even resistant pupils. What does "pupil" mean? The word used for a pupil in the classroom and the pupil of the eye are derived from the same Latin root meaning a "little boy" or a "little girl" and suggests immaturity. However, the choice of the ancient Greeks of the word "pupil" to identify the opening in the center of the iris that determines the amount of light that enters the eye is most revealing. Could this mean that the teacher is the guiding light that determines how much the student sees up close and how far they can see in the future? If the teacher is the source of light and the amount of light that enters the eye is controlled by the muscular diaphragm surrounding the pupil of the eye, then the student has some control over what they permit themselves to see or learn. Teachers who do not effectively teach contribute to the immaturity of a generation and may be responsible for many of the problems that society has to face because of undeveloped judgment and/or acts of undisciplined individuals.

Inductive or Self-Study

Inductive study, at times understood to be self-study, is a

method-path to learning. Method is based on the Greek word *methodos,* which literally means "a way or path of transit." Method implies orderly, logical, and effective arrangement and denotes either an abstraction or a concrete procedure. Method is a way of doing things, which carefully maintains and fosters conditions conducive to understanding and growth.

Inductive or self-study is a learner following a specific plan to understand what is meant by the written and spoken words and the way the words are put together. One may better interpret what is written by following the procedure self-evident in the seven words or constructs below. This hermeneutical process is systematic and rewarding.

1. **See** - observe the link between subject and object.
2. **Inquire** - inquisitiveness is required to find the meaning.
3. **Answer** - re-creating the attitude or intent of the writer is a source of answers.
4. **Summarize** - integrate and summarize to discover message.
5. **Evaluate** - determine the local or universal value of what is written.
6. **Apply** – a universal or specific application of the facts presented.
7. **Associate** - written passages must be associated with each other and with extra-source data to develop the ultimate correlation.

Building Blocks in Understanding

Whether one is reading a book or listening to a lecture, there are four major building blocks to understanding a written or spoken message. (1) **Terms** - the distinct use of a or word group of words. (2) **Structure** - the relationship and inter-relationship between words or groups of words. (3) **General literary forms** - the format used to communicate the message. And (4) **Atmosphere** - the underlying tone or spirit communicated by a written or spoken message.

Education Has Come Full Circle

Education has come full circle since John Milton Gregory (1822-1998) observed that **the best classroom was nothing more than a good teacher on one end of a log and a pupil on the other.** In addition to his seven laws of teaching, Gregory had other timeless insights with universal application. Not realizing the impact of the future technology on education, Gregory's statement about the log with a teacher on one end and the pupil on the other has direct application to the present D.I.A.L. System (Directed Internet Assisted Learning used by Oxford Graduate School in Tennessee and OASIS University in Trinidad as well as other technically advanced institutions. In D.I.A.L. a student uploads assignments to an Internet site and the professor logs into the sight and evaluates and grades the assignments. This interactive process is literally Gregory's log coming full circle.

CHAPTER TEN

Faculty Directed and Independent Learning

Pointed in the Right Direction

In this age of distance education there is still a need for the teacher, tutor, or learning leader. Although learning is self discovery, students normally need a guide on the journey to excellence. Mature students may need less hands-on instructions than young, but the need for a learning leader is still present. In fact, part of the task of the teaching/learning process is keeping students from becoming dependent on the teacher. Most of the time, motivated students simply need to be pointed in the right direction or occasionally reminded of the logical steps in a methodology and they become self-sufficient learners. Normally, this can be done with written instructions or with a few moments of teacher/ student interface. At other times, students need and want the stimulation of a group working together to maintain sufficient momentum to complete a subject or a program of study. Also, there are occasions when new material is covered or specialized competency is required to handle difficult material and a few words from a competent teacher are welcomed.

Together with a number of other factors, a primary task of a teacher is to stimulate interest, arouse a spirit of inquiry and get the learner involved in the process of discovery regardless of age and maturity. As a rule a good teacher should avoid telling students anything they could discover on their own. The instructor must have full command of the subject matter at hand with relevant experience to encourage students to steer carefully through the learning curves ahead. Unless there is confidence in the teacher, participation in the learning process will be less than satisfactory. One essential factor is the knowledge and preparation of the teacher. The learner will pay close attention to what is being taught by a competent teacher.

As the learner gives heed to the teacher, they move beyond hearing words to the level of listening that requires analysis and action. The responsibility for this attention is on the teacher. Unless self-motivation occurs on the part of the student there will be little learning. Unless the student can reproduce in his/her own words the facts related to the instruction, there was a failure to communicate. Failure is usually a teacher problem with some blame placed on the curriculum, the educational environment, and the deportment of other students. Discipline in the classroom and the learning environment must be under the command of the teacher. Otherwise the failure to learn will be blamed on the student rather than the teacher. If no learning occurs, there was no teaching. The student moved through a process. At first the felling is one of dependence; then an attitude of counter-dependence erupts and the student begins to feel they can function on their own. This leads to a period of independence and then matures into a kind of interdependence where teacher and learner work together to achieve excellence in the teaching/learning process.

Experiential Learning Methods

Experiential learning methods are redesigned to produce individuals who are motivated, assertive, adaptable, effective, and communicative. These are the kind of adult professionals required in a technological world subject to increasing rates of change. It is firmly believed by experts in the field, that experimental methodology exists to develop individuals who have a comprehensive grasp of analytic cognitive skills and discipline-based knowledge.

The literature also assures that this will not be at the expense of affective, cognitive, synthesizing, integrative and practical skills. Actually, experiential learners are able to use self-directed learning methods to enhance their educational process. Knowles (1984) argued that mature learners have a deep psychological need for self-direction. Traditional approaches to education tend to provide poor articulation between what is learned in the classroom and its application in the real world. Mature and advanced learners need to use self-direction as an effective strategy for learning in their professional workplace. Often the classroom model increases the perception that what occurs is simply an academic exercise with little or no relationship to real life demands. Theory and facts covered in the classroom and normally not used in the life of an adult professional. Consequently, an mature educational model must be a model of self-directed learning.

Advantages and Outcomes of Self-Direction

The concept is complex but the advantages and outcomes of a self-directed model enhance any effort at further education for mature students. Brockett and Hiemstra (1991) dealt with the value of the mature learner accepting ever increasing responsibility for decisions associated with the learning process. Candy (1988) claimed that self-direction had been used to indicate learning outside formal settings and as learner control over instruction. The latter is perhaps the most important aspect of self-directed learning because it represents the ultimate state of learner autonomy (Mocker and Spear 1982). The strategy is to enhance the educational process to the extent the learner accepts the responsibility for planning, implementing and evaluating learning. In such an approach, the learner has more control of the actual learning situation, deciding what and how to learn, and whether to continue or abandon the specific learning activity. Ultimately, the learner is able to determine the adequacy of the outcomes.

Personal Responsibility vs. Self-Directed Learning

There are two mediating variables between personal responsibility and self-direction in learning. They are the learning situation and the characteristics of the learner. The learning situation has four phases: (1) **Initiation.** The purpose of the situation is recognized and the outcomes defined for the learner. (2) **Planning.** The formulation of the steps to be taken, the resources required, and the criteria to be satisfied are articulated. (3) **Managing.** A review of the learning activities is made, the data analyzed and conclusions for further developments drawn. (4) **Evaluation.** Decisions relating to the nature of achievements in phase-one objectives are made and the implications for further learning are defined.

Experiential Learning Methods

Experiential learning methods are redesigned to produce individuals who are motivated, assertive, adaptable, communicative, and effective. These are the kind of students required in a technological world subject to increasing rates of change. It is firmly believed by experts in the field, that experimental methodology exists to develop individuals who have a comprehensive grasp of analytic cognitive skills and discipline-based knowledge.

The literature also assures that this will not be at the expense of affective, cognitive, synthesizing, integrative and practical skills. Actually, experiential learners are able to use self-directed learning methods to enhance the learning process.   Knowles (1984) argued that mature students had a deep psychological need for self-direction. Traditional approaches to education tend to provide poor articulation between what is learned in the classroom and its application in the real world. Mature students need to use self-direction as an effective strategy for learning in real time. Often the classroom model increases the perception that what occurs is simply an academic exercise with little or no relationship to real life demands. Beyond the basics and essential elements of a subject, mature students should be encouraged to make life-applications using their self-directed skills.

Advantages and Outcomes of Self-Direction

The concept is complex but the advantages and outcomes of a self-directed model enhance teaching/learning process. Brockett and Hiemstra (1991) dealt with the value of the mature learner accepting ever increasing responsibility for decisions associated with the learning process. Candy (1988) claimed that self-direction had been used to indicate learning outside formal settings and as learner control over instruction. The latter is perhaps the most important aspect of self-directed learning because it represents the ultimate state of learner autonomy (Mocker and Spear 1982). The strategy is to enhance the educational process to the extent the learner accepts the responsibility for planning, implementing and evaluating learning. In such an approach, the learner has more control of the actual learning situation, deciding what and how to learn, and whether to continue or abandon the specific learning activity. Ultimately, the learner is able to determine the adequacy of the outcomes.

Hammond and Collins (1991) claimed that the self-directed model changed the power relationships so that the learner and the teacher share control. In this way, the learner is required to accept a significant part of the responsibility for planning, securing resources, and implementing the learning experience. This certainly supports the early construct that the teacher's task was "to excite and direct the self-activity of the learner and as a rule tell them nothing they can learn for themselves. The learner also becomes involved in the evaluation of the process. (Herbeson 1991)

Experiential Learning refers to a spectrum of practices and ideologies. (1) Experiential learning is primarily the assessing of learning from life and work experience as a basis for creating new routes into higher education. (2) The need to focus on experiential learning as a basis for change in the purpose, structures and curricula of educational opportunities. (3) A need to emphasize experiential learning as a basis for social change and community action. And (4) Experiential learning is related to personal growth and development that approaches the increase of self-awareness and competency.

Central to experiential learning activities are student involvement, learner control, and the relationship of the learning task to real life obligations. While traditional learning focuses on a product and knowledge, experiential learning is directed towards the process. The end product may be increased understanding, subsequent change or a plan for the future. Essential to experiential learning, is a significant experience, which plays an instrumental role in the learning process. Situated between the initial experience and the subsequent outcome is some plan of mental activity, be it generalization, conceptualization or reflection. The end may be personal or practical means of empowerment.

Experiential learning should hasten social change, learning by doing, personal or professional development and/or increased competency in some area of life. It is directed toward a holistic education and assessment procedures should address each of the cognitive, affective and psychomotor domain dimensions.

Baud, Cohen and Walker (1993) developed five propositions to assist adult educators in developing effective experiential learning opportunities and to assist the integrity of the professional practice of faculty. (1) Experience is the foundation of, and the stimulus for learning. (2) Learners actively construct their experience. (3) Learning is a holistic process. (4) Learning is socially and culturally constructed. (5) Learning is influenced by the socio-emotional context in which it occurs.

Faculty Directed Learning Model

In order for the faculty directed model to work two aspects of the teacher/learner environment must be present. First, the teacher must demonstrate intellectual excitement about the subject at hand. Second, the teacher must develop an interpersonal rapport with the students that goes beyond positional authority.   Demonstrated personal influence must be present in the classroom. This requires clarity of communication and the creation of a positive learning environment that excites and directs the learner on the path to understanding.

Academic study in theory is both intellectual and rational. In reality, the educational process is a highly emotional and interpersonal practice and requires a combination of intellectual excitement and interpersonal rapport. There must be an affinity relationship between teacher and learner. This is a trust relationship with firm reliance on the integrity and ability of the teacher and a concern for learning expressed by the student. The faculty directed learning model cannot work without integrity and trust.

Synergogic Teaching Designs

In addition to class-based learning under the authority of a teacher and the self-study process of inductive study, there are synergogic designs that permit adults to learn from each other. At the end of this chapter is a general independent study mechanism to create a virtual classroom laboratory. Below are four designs where students can work together as a team to foster learning. They are Team Effectiveness Design, Team-Member Teaching Design, Performance Judging Design, and Clarifying Attitudes Design. A brief word about these designs could whet one's appetite for innovation in learning.

Team Effectiveness Design

In the Team Effectiveness Design, each of a team's learners assesses his/her knowledge before team discussion. After an initial review or pre-study of multiple-choice objective content instrument, team members then work together to reach consensus on the best answer to each question. Members present their choices and reasons for them and learn about other members' choices. Since the task is to achieve consensus, participants have the opportunity to exchange information, to explain their reasoning, to assess the reasons and evidence provided by others, and to use logic in weighing pros and cons of each alternative as the best answer.

Later, in general sessions, objective scoring enables team members to assess their individual work and the team's consensus answers are scored for comparison with other teams. An answer key or a lead teacher with the key provides a rationale for each answer, which further aids team members in understanding why answers, according to the key, are regarded as the most valid. Team members then use an evaluation period to assess how well they worked as a team and to plan how to increase their effectiveness. Of particular interest are those cases in which one member offered the correct answer but was unable to achieve team consensus for that answer. Open and highly involving discussions usually result from team members' analyzing why they did not agree on the correct answer when it was proposed. This design is useful for presenting subject matter that requires students to learn facts and data and to deduce principles or consequences. (Mouton 1984).

Team-Member Teaching Design

In the Team-Member Teaching Design, participants are responsible for learning an assigned portion of the subject matter and teaching it to the others. Once each member's part is fitted with the others, the entire body of knowledge is known to all. This design somewhat resembles a jigsaw puzzle. At the beginning, all the parts are present but unassembled. The learning design provides the structure by which the parts can be put together so that the whole picture is visible and each participant understands it. Team-member teaching, in which the teaching is done by a team's members, is not to be confused with team teaching, in which two or more instructors share responsibility for a group of students.

This Team-Member design requires that the subject matter be subdivided and a part assigned as pre-study to each member. When the team assembles, the member with the first part teaches that material to the others then other members in turn teach their parts. A comprehensive review of the material is administered to assess each participant's understanding. An answer key or a member with the key provides the expert rationale for each item and helps learners understand whatever questions each may have missed. In a subsequent brief critique period, team members assess how well each seems to have learned and communicated the assigned subject matter, and members suggest how individuals could increase their effectiveness. This design is similar to the Team Effectiveness Design and is most useful for aiding the learners to acquire information, facts, and data. These two designs may be used in combination to add variety to the learning environment. (Mouton 1984)

Classroom Laboratory Design for Independent Study

Data were gathered from English and European educational practices in an effort to place the procedures in the context of mature learners. These instructional and tutorial procedures are a result of the efforts to adapt these procedures to the context of education outside of Europe. Consequently, the theoretical and taxonomically constructed instructional methodology and the tutorial procedure form a model created from adaptations derived from an eclectic process. This methodology is used to create classroom dynamics for independent study. Authors of the various texts are to be viewed as persons. The author of the primary text should be viewed as the principal source of course content. Authors of the secondary texts should be viewed as the two best informed members of the class who will agree and disagree with the principal source. Authors of the general bibliography form the balance of the class. The student's present knowledge of the subject matter becomes a source of interaction with the authors to complete classroom dynamics of this sixteen-step plan known as a Virtual Classroom Laboratory Design

Virtual Classroom Laboratory Design

1. Using the course description, select a primary text and two secondary texts for the course for approval by the Faculty Advisor and Faculty designated for the course.
2. Develop a brief supplemental bibliography of three-to-six volumes related specifically to the course. These are in addition to the primary and secondary texts. In some select cases, a general bibliography of the field of study would be acceptable.
3. Make an initial evaluation of the primary and secondary texts. Using only the title, table of contents, preface, introduction, publisher's blurb, glossary, foreword, or afterword, write a one-page explanation of the purpose of each text.
4. Read the primary and secondary texts carefully and write a brief paragraph on each chapter identifying the major themes and/or elements.

[5-8: Working with the most foundational chapter]

5. Select from the primary text the chapter most foundational to the study as described in the course description. Defend the choice in writing. Study the selected chapter; note important topics; write a summary/ analysis or sentence outline of the chapter.
6. Survey the secondary texts for additional material that supports the data from the foundational chapter. Delineate this additional material.
7. Survey the secondary texts for material that does not agree with the data in the foundational chapter. Delineate this variant material.
8. Review the supplemental bibliography for additive and variant material with relation to the foundational chapter of the primary text. Delineate this additional material, which supports the primary text and that which is at variance.

[9-12: Working with the most conclusive/implemental chapter]

9. Select the chapter in the primary text that is most conclusive or implemental to the course. Defend this choice. Write a summary/ analysis or sentence outline of the chapter.
10. Survey the secondary texts for additional material that supports the data from the conclusive or implemental chapter. Delineate this material.
11. Survey the secondary texts for material that does not agree with the data in the conclusive or implemental chapter of the primary text. Delineate this additional material, which supports the primary text and that which is at variance.
12. Review the supplemental bibliography for additive and variant material with relation to the conclusive/implemental chapter of the primary text. Delineate this additional material, which supports the primary text and that which is at variance.
13. Select from the primary text the chapter most applicable to your life and/or career. Defend the choice in writing. Study the selected chapter noting what is important. Write a summary/analysis or sentence outline of this chapter.

[13-14 Personalizing the topic.]

14. Write a one-page explanation of ways you may use what you have learned from this study in your professional and/or personal life.
15. Evaluate the texts and the bibliography. Write a brief evaluation of the primary and secondary texts noting their strengths and weaknesses. Given the opportunity, how would you improve the bibliography you used in this course?
16. Compose an examination of 50 questions covering this study. Write 20 true and false questions and indicate the correct answer. Write 10 fill in the blank questions and designate the correct answer. Write 10 matching questions and indicate the correct answer. Write 10 short essay

questions and write a paragraph or two to answer each. Be balanced, complete, clear, and specific. (This assortment may be rearranged by the instructor.)

When the 16 assignments are completed, submit them to the the appropriate instructor for evaluation. Present the primary and secondary texts if so instructed when the bibliography is approved.

—Source: Green, Hollis L. (1984) -- The theoretical and taxonomically constructed instructional methodology and the tutorial procedure form a model created from adaptations derived from an eclectic process.

APPENDIX A

Study and Review Questions

1   **Compare** Andragogy and Pedagogy.
2   **Delineate** some accepted constructs of mature learners.
3   **Why** is the learner considered self-directed in the Andragogy model?
4   **What** is structure and distance in education?
5   **Discuss** the advantage of the CPM/PERT approach to educational delivery.
6   **Discuss** the problem with the normal grading system.
7   **What** is the significance of a nonsectarian, nonprofit, non-discriminatory education program?
8   **What** is the difference between a complicated and a sophisticated system?
9   **What** happens when two or more forces work together?
10 **Discuss** the Greek meaning of cybernetics.
11 **Why** is there still a need for teachers?
12 **What** is the primary task of the teacher?
13 **Evaluate** Gregory's seven laws of teaching.
14 **Name** the design that permits students to learn from one another?
15 **Enumerate** the ways a Cognitive Taxonomy is of value to a teacher.
16 **How** is the Affective Taxonomy useful to educators?

APPENDIX B

Bibliography

Allen, K., & Cherrey, C. (2000). *Systemic Leadership: Enriching the Meaning of Our Work*. Lanham, MD: University Press of America.

Arvey, R.D., Rotundo, M., Johnson, W., Zhang, Z., & McGue, M. (2006). The determinants of leadership role occupancy: Genetic and personality factors. *The Leadership Quarterly*, 17, 1-20.

Avolio, B. J. (1999). *Full leadership development: Building the vital forces in organizations*. Thousand Oaks, CA: Sage.

Barge, J. Kevin. (1994). *Leadership: Communication Skills for Organizations and Groups*. New York: St. Martin's Press.

Barna, George. (2001) *The Power of Team Leadership: Achieving Success Through Shared Responsibility*. New York: Random House Inc.

Bass B. & Avolio, B. (1994). *Improving Organizational effectiveness through transformational leadership*. Thousand Oaks, CA. Sage Publications.

Bass, B. (1990). *Bass & Stogdill's Handbook of Leadership: Theory, Research, and Managerial Applications*. New York, NY: Free Press.

Bass, B. (1997). Does the transactional-transformational leadership paradigm transcend organizational and national boundaries? *American Psychologist* 52 (2) 130-139.

Bass, B. (1998). *Transformational leadership: Industry, military, and educational impact*. Mahwah, NJ: Erlbaum Associates.

Bass, B.M. & Bass, R. (2008). *The Bass handbook of leadership: Theory, research, and managerial applications (4th ed.)*. New York: Free Press.

Blake, R.; Mouton, J. (1964). *The Managerial Grid: The Key to Leadership Excellence*. Houston: Gulf Publishing Co.

Blanchard, Kenneth and Norman Vincent Peale. (1988). *The Power of Ethical Management*. New York: William Morrow and Company.

Bloom B. S. (1956). *Taxonomy of Educational Objectives, Handbook I: The Cognitive Domain.* New York: David McKay Co Inc.

Brockett, R. G. and Hiemstra, R. (1991) *Self-Direction in Adult Learning: Perspectives on Theory, Research, and Practice,* London and New York: Routledge.

Bryson, J.M., & Crosby, B.C. (1992). *Leadership for the Common Good: Tackling Public Problems in a Shared-Power World.* San Francisco, CA: Jossey-Bass Publishers.

Burns, J. M. (1978) *Leadership,* New York: Harper and Row

Burns, J. M. (2003). *Transforming leadership: A new pursuit of happiness.* NY: Atlantic Monthly Press.

Candy, Philip C. 1991. *Self-Direction for Lifelong Learning.* San Francisco:

Chrislip, D.D., & Larson, C.E. (1994). *Collaborative Leadership: How Citizens and Civic Leaders Can Make a Difference.* San Francisco, CA: Jossey-Bass Publishers.

Coles, R. (2000). *Lives of Moral Leadership.* New York, NY: Random House.

Conger, J.A., & Pearce, C.L. (2003). *Shared Leadership: Reframing the Hows and Whys of Leadership.* Thousand Oaks, CA: Sage Publications.

Cranton, Patnca. 1994. *Understanding and Promoting Transformative Learning.* San Francisco: Jossey-Bass Publishers.

Crosby, B.C. (1999). *Leadership for Global Citizenship: Building Transnational Community.* Thousand Oaks, CA: Sage Publications.

Dave, R. H. (1975). *Developing and Writing Behavioural Objectives.* (R J Armstrong, ed.) Educational Innovators Press.

Day, C., Harris, A. & Hadfield, M. (2001). Challenging the orthodoxy of effective school leadership, *Leadership in Education* 4 (1), 39-56

Drath, W. (2001). *The Deep Blue Sea: Rethinking the Source of Leadership.* San Francisco, CA: Jossey-Bass Publishers.

Drath, W., & Palus, C. (1994). Making Common Sense: Leadership as Meaning Making in a Community of Practice. Greensboro, NC: *Center for Creative Leadership.*

Drucker, F. Peter. (1995). *Managing in a Time of Great Change.* New York: Penguin Group.

Erickson, C. H. 1962. *Childhood and Society,* 2nd edition, rev. New York:

Evers, C. W., & Lakomski, G. (2000). *Doing educational administration: A theory of administrative practice.* NY: Pergamon.

Fleishman, E. A. (2000). Leadership skills for a changing world solving complex social problems. *The Leadership Quarterly,* 11, 11-35.

Foster, R., & Young, J. (2004). Leadership: Current themes from the educational literature. *The CAP Journal(12)*3, 29-30.

Fullan, M. (2001). *Leading in a culture of change.* San Francisco: Jossey-Bass.

Gardner, H. (1995). *Leading Minds: An Anatomy of Leadership.* New York, NY: Basic Books.

George, Bill. (2003) *Authentic Leadership: Rediscovering the Secrets to Creating Lasting Value.* Valley Forge: Jossey-Bass.

Giles, C. (2006). Transformational Leadership in Challenging Urban Elementary Schools: A role For Parental Involvement? *University of Buffalo, The State University of New York.*

Giuliani, Rudolph W. (2002). *Leadership.* New York: Miramax.

Green, Hollis L. (2007) *Sympathetic Leadership Cybernetics*, Nashville. GlobalEdAdvancePress.

Green, Hollis L. (2007) *Why Christianity Fails in America*, Nashville. GlobalEdAdvancePress

Green, Hollis L. (2008) *Interpreting an Author's Words.* Nashville, GlobalEdAdvancePress.

Green, Hollis L. (2009) *Remesdial and Surrogate Parenting in the Custodial Arena.* GloblEdAdvancePress.

Green, Hollis L. (2010). *The Evergreen Devotional New Testament Second Edition*, Nashville, Post-Gutenberg Books

Green, Hollis L. (2010). Designing Valid Research. Nashville, GlobalEdAdvancePress.

Greenleaf, R.K. (1977). *Servant Leadership: A journey into the nature of legitimate power and greatness.* Mahwah, NJ: Paulist Press.

Gutek, Gerald, (1988) *Philosophies, Ideologies, and Theories of Education*, Allyn & Bacon.

Hallinger, P. (2003). Leading educational change: Reflections on the practice of instructional and transformational leadership. *Cambridge Journal of Education, 33* (3), 329-351.

Hammond M, Collins R (1991) *Self-directed learning: Critical Practice.* Kogan Page,

Harrow, Anita (1972) *A taxonomy of psychomotor domain: a guide for developing behavioral objectives.* New York: David McKay.

Hastings, Wayne A. *Trust Me: Developing a Leadership Style People Will Follow.* New York: Random House Inc, 2004

.Heifetz, R. & Linsky, M. (2002). *Leadership on the Line: Staying Alive through the Dangers of Leading.* Boston, MA: Harvard Business School Press.

Hemphill, John K. (1949). *Situational Factors in Leadership.* Columbus: Ohio State University Bureau of Educational Research.

Herbeson, E. (1991). Self-directed learning and level of education.

Australian Journal of Adult and Community Education.

Hersey, Paul; Blanchard, Ken; Johnson, D. (2008). *Management of Organizational Behavior: Leading Human Resources* (9th ed.). Upper Saddle River, NJ: Pearson Education.

Israel, M. and Hay, I. (2006) *Research Ethics for Social Scientists: Between Ethical Conduct and Regulatory Compliance.* London: Sage.

Judge, T. A., Piccolo, R. F. (2004) Transformational and Transactional Leadership: a meta-nalytic test of their relative validity. *UFla.* Gainesville

Kaczmarski, K. & Cooperrider, David. (1997). Construction Leadership in the Global Relational Age. *Organization & Environment*, 10(3), 235-258

Kaplan, T. (1997). *Crazy for Democracy: Women in Grassroots Movements.* New York, NY: Routledge

Kenneth D. Bailey (2006). Living systems theory and social entropy theory. *Systems Research and Behavioral Science, 22,* 291-300.

Kenneth D. Bailey, (1994). *Sociology and the new systems theory: Toward a theoretical synthesis.* Albany, NY: SUNY Press.

Kouzes, J., and Posner, B. (2007). *The Leadership Challenge.* CA: Jossey Bass.

Krathwohl, D. R., Bloom, B. S., & Masia, B. B. (1973). *Taxonomy of Educational Objectives, the Classification of Educational Goals. Handbook II: Affective Domain.* New York: David McKay Co., Inc.

Leithwood, K. & Jantzi, D. (1999). The effects of transformational leadership on organizational conditions and student engagement with school. *Journal of Educational Administration* 38 (2), 112-129.

Leithwood, K. (Ed.) (2000). *Understanding schools as intelligent systems.* CT: JAI Press

Leithwood, K., Jantzi, D. & Steinbach, R. (1999). *Changing leadership for changing times.* Buckingham, UK: Open University Press.

Lewis, Phillip V. (1996) *Transformational Leadership.* Nashville: Broadman & Holman.

Lippitt, R., Watson, J. and Westley, B. (1958).*The Dynamics of Planned Change.* New York: Harcourt, Brace and World.

Marks, M. Printy, S. (2003). Principal leadership and school performance: An integration of transformational and instructional leadership. *Educational Administration Quarterly* 39 (3), 370-397.

Marshall, Tom. (2003). *Understanding Leadership.* Grand Rapids: Baker.

McLuhan, Marshall (1967).*The Medium is the Message.* London: Allen Lane

Meindl, J.R., Ehrlich, S.B. and Dukerich, J.M. (1985). The Romance of
        Leadership. *Administrative Science Quarterly*, 30(1), 78-102
Miller, James Grier, (1978). *Living systems*. New York: McGraw-Hill.
Mocker and Spears (1982) Adult learning in Nonformal Institutions,
        ERIC Digest.
O'Toole, James.(1995). *Leading Change: Overcoming the Ideology of
        Comfort and The Tyranny of Custom*. San Francisco: Jossey-
        Bass Publishers.
Palus, C.J., & Horth, D.M. (1996). Leading Creatively: The Art of Making
        Sense. *Journal of Aesthetic Education*, 30(4), 53-68.
Pastor, J.C. (1998). *The Social Construction of Leadership: A Semantic
        and Social Network Analysis of Social Representations of
        Leadership*. Ann Arbor, MI: UMI
Pfeiffer, J. William and Jones, John E. (1974), A Handbook of Structural
        Experiences for Human Relations Training. *Leadership Center*:
        HM 134
Pohl, Michael. (2000). *Learning to Think, Thinking to Learn: Models
        and Strategies to Develop a Classroom Culture of Thinking*.
        Cheltenham, Vic.: Hawker Brownlow.
Rickards, T., & Moger, S., (2000) 'Creative leadership processes in
        project team development: An alternative to Tuckman's stage
        model', *British Journal of Management*, Part 4, pp273-283
Rickards, T., & Moger,S.T., (1999). *Handbook for creative team leaders*,
        Aldershot, Hants: Gower.
Robbins, Stephen. (2003). *Organizational Behavior. 10th ed*. Upper
        Saddle River, NJ: Prentice Hall.
Robnett, B. (1996). African-American Women in the Civil rights
        Movement, 1954-1965: Gender, Leadership, and Micro
        Mobilization. *American Journal of Sociology*, 101(6), 1661-
        1693.
Rost, J. (1991). *Leadership for the Twenty-first Century*. New York, NY:
        Praeger.
Sanders, J.E.(3rd), Hopkins, W.E. & Geroy, G.D. (2003). From
        transactional to transcendental: toward an integrated theory of
        leadership. *Journal of Leadership and Organizational Studies*,
        9(4), pp. 21-31.
Sanders, J. Oswald. (1967) *Spiritual Leadership*. Chicago: Moody.
Schaller, Lyle. (1972). *The Change Agent*. Nashville: Abingdon.
Shook, John. (2000) *Dewey's Empirical Theory of Knowledge and
        Reality*. The Vanderbilt Library of American Philosophy.
Simpson E. J. (1972). *The Classification of Educational Objectives in the
        Psychomotor Domain*. Washington, DC: Gryphon House.
Sims, H., Jr., & Lorenzi, P. (1992). *The New Leadership Paradigm: Social*

Learning and Cognition in Organizations. Newbury Park, CA: Sage Publications.

Sleeper, R.W. (2001). *The Necessity of Pragmatism: John Dewey's Conception of Philosophy.* Introduction by Tom Burke. University of Illinois Press.

Soder, Roger. (2001). *The Language of Leadership.* Valley Forge: John Wiley and Sons.

Swanson, G.A. and Miller, James Grier. (1989) *Measurement and interpretation in Accounting: A Living Systems Theory Approach.* New York: Qurum Books.

Swanson, G.A., and Green, Hollis L. (1991, 2004) *Understanding Scientific Research: An Introductory Handbook for the Social Professions.* Nashville: Oxford/ACRSS Press.

Tate, T. (2003). Servant leadership for schools and youth programs. Reclaiming Children and Youth: *The Journal of Strength-based Interventions,* 12, 33-39.

Tuckman, Bruce W. (1965) 'Developmental Sequence in Small Groups', Psychological Bulletin, Volume 63, Number 6, pp. 384 99, *American Psychological Association*

Vanderslice, V. (1988). Separating Leadership from Leaders: An Assessment of the Effect of Leader and Follower Roles in Organizations. *Human Relations,* 41 (9), 677-696.

Westbrook, Robert B. (1991). *John Dewey and American Democracy.* Cornell University Press.

White, Alasdair A. K. (2008). *From Comfort Zone to Performance Management.* White & MacLean Publishing.

Wlodkowski, R. J. *1998. Enhancing Adult Motivation to Learn.* San Francisco, Jossey-Bass Publications.

Zaccaro, S. J. (2007). Trait-based perspectives of leadership. *American Psychologist,* 62, 6-16.

Appendix C

PostScript:

The Use of Transformational Concepts

The author affirms that the vision, transformational concepts and constructs presented in this book are transferable and could be used throughout the field of education. They were used by a Task Force (1974-1981) to establish Oxford Graduate School/ACRSS (1981) to meet an educational need in the USA. The same Task Force data and twenty years experience were used to initiate O.A.S.I.S. University (2002) to deal with Caribbean issues and are being utilized to meet a need in the Jewish Community (2010) through Yeshiva Torah Institute.

PostScript One

Excerpts from a speech to the ACTT –
Accrediting Commission of Trinidad and Tobago
Hollis L. Green, ThD, PhD
July 03, 2009

The Value of an Interdisciplinary Education

Greetings to all: My subject today concerns the value of an interdisciplinary education. This is the ability to view a subject or phenomenon through an integration of several disciplines and includes an effort to overcome prejudice and discrimination that improves mutual understanding among peoples and cultural groups.

The best advice about such personal development and education came from Col. Creed Bates, U.S. Army. Learning that I had decided not to make Military Service my career, Col. Bates called me to his office, I saluted, reported and was asked to be seated. Looking straight at me, Col. Bates said, "Don't think you can go to school for 4, 5, or 6 years and ever communicate with anyone. What you need to do is go to school part-time and work full time with people. You must stay in touch with the real world; not get lost in academia."

Out of this advice came my interest in interdisciplinary education with an alternative delivery system for mature students living in the real world of family and work difficulties.

In 1974 I selected 100 professionals to work on a Task Force for seven years to decide how we could change the world in our life time. After considering many options that included boys and girls clubs, scouting programs, working with the YMCA, planting churches and doing missionary work, we decided to start a graduate program in education. Why this? It was determined that the other programs would take 20 to 40 years before an individual could develop the influence to make intentional changes in their environment. The Task Force decided to engage mature well-educated adults with an already determined professional influence to expedite social change theory.

The Task Force looked at the Yeshiva project, a Jewish model, that originally endorsed Jewish professors in various universities, and all courses taken from these approved professors could be transferred to the Yeshiva project for academic credit. We thought the educational brokerage idea was good, but realized that most people do not stick together or cooperate with each other as well as the Jewish people do. The Task Force continued to search for a workable model.

The University of Oxford was an educational brokerage system with multiple colleges loosely connected with the University. It had worked for over 800 years with universal appeal. Traveling extensively in England with a public relations and corporate development project (Associated Institutional Development, known as, AID, Ltd. (1962-1974), provided access and knowledge of the Oxbridge system and Task Force ideas were discussed with key people in the UK.

With University connections in the US, Canada, UK, Europe, Asia, and South Africa, a graduate program was initiated with approval from the Tennessee Higher Education Commission. With their blessing and assistance, the Task Force founded Oxford Graduate School in Tennessee (1981) and selected me as the founding President. The objectives were to put principles and values back into business and industry and generally integrate morality and ethics in society.

(www.ogs.edu)

We wanted busy professionals who desired to advance their academic standing and participate in a global effort to change the world while maintaining a close connection with their career and family. The intention was to develop an educational brokerage and connect with several colleges and universities around the world to build an educational model that would reach individuals in the social professions.   We developed a UK connection in Oxford, the American Centre for Religion/Society Studies (ACRSS) that continues to operate in England as a "poor man's Rhodes project" to introduce graduate students to the English model of reading and research during J-Terms.

However, when Dr. Swanapoo, our key contact at the University of South Africa (Pretoria) died suddenly, it was decided to work only with the UK and the Tennessee based free-standing graduate school and put the global expansion effort on hold until more funds were available. During the next 20 years we recruited students from the USA and 27 countries including the Caribbean region and offered master's and doctorates in sociological integration with an emphasis on social research.

Caribbean Expansion

There was a problem in the Caribbean of the 42 students recruited only 3 graduated. It was determined that those 3 received more personal dialogue and support from the faculty; therefore, it became obvious to serve the Caribbean, we must institute a better dialogue and support system. We looked at St. Thomas, USVI, St. Kitts, and in 2001 considered Trinidad and Tobago. In a sponsored Team Oxford luncheon in Trinidad in 2001, 33 prospective students attended, but only Raymond Boca was interested in going to Tennessee for graduate work. After the meeting, Paratan Balloo called and expressed an interest. I spoke at a local college and briefly met with Steve Mohammed who was willing to continue his graduate work in Tennessee, but that was only 3 out of 35. Nearly 90 percent of the students were not willing to leave Trinidad to further their education. What could be done?

When Steve Mohammed met with me for more information, he brought with him Subesh Ramjattan, who sat patiently as I explained the doctoral program in Tennessee.. At the end of our conversation, I turned to Subesh and asked, "Did God send you here to help me or can I do something for you, or could we do something together?" Subesh answered, "I am building a compound above the University; come see if you can use it?" We chartered O.A.S.I.S. in 2002 using the Anapausis campus and during the first Term Core, October, 2002, O.A.S.I.S had a site visit from CORD. We had established the first free-standing, not-for-profit graduate program in Trinidad that was to be controlled and operated by Caribbean personnel.

Now the rest of the story!

Using the basic educational philosophy and graduate curriculum developed by the Task Force and two decades of experience with social professionals at Oxford Graduate School, O.A.S.I.S. was ready to serve Trinidad and Tobago and the Caribbean Region with government approval.

The Founders of O.A.S.I.S. had a multicultural Judeo-Christian heritage similar to those principles and precepts that support jurisprudence and most institutions of the West. O.A.S.I.S. is committed to develop programs that provide equal access to education for all, regardless of gender, religion, race, color or ethnic origin. The institution respects the rights of all individuals to observe customarily recognized religious holidays throughout the academic year provided the institution is notified in writing prior to the specified holiday not scheduled as public holidays.

The Board, Administration and Faculty are committed to provide to Trinidad and Tobago and the wider Caribbean Region affordable interdisciplinary educational programs to serve mature adult learners that reflect the value of global transformation and understanding, multicultural awareness, emerging knowledge and skills and international exchange. This perspective forms the premise for further development of the academic programs, support services and resources for O.A.S.I.S.

(www.oasisedu.org)

O.A.S.I.S. Mission

A private tertiary institution founded in 2002, the initial campus is located in St. Augustine, Trinidad and structured to serve the Caribbean Region. Although it is small; the reach is global. The institutional mission is to develop leaders through relevant interdisciplinary academic studies who will positively influence their own environment through leadership and social research; thereby, fulfilling the academic goals of discovery, dissemination, preservation and creative application of knowledge.

The academic program of O.A.S.I.S. University is known as the Institute of Higher Learning and offers credit and non-credit continuing education, undergraduate and graduate courses and degree programs. Breadth, depth, and application of learning are the basis for competencies in all subject areas. Advanced studies require both practical and expert knowledge and rigorous scholarship. All applicants are objectively assessed. Applicants with varying backgrounds and levels of academic proficiency must demonstrate potential for academic success.

Faculty and staff will guide students to academic achievement through a transformational philosophy encompassing diverse learning processes of major global tertiary institutions. The objective is to create a collaborative model for the Caribbean Community and assure an interactive individualized educational delivery system for mature, serious students. The curriculum emphasizes the Judeo-Christian values common to the Caribbean and will build on these through culturally specific adaptations and processes.

 The entire community of scholars participates in an ongoing assessment, planning, and evaluation process to improve and demonstrate institutional effectiveness in the following areas: governance, academic programs, public service functions, support services, and administrative operations. The institution will have fulfilled its purpose if its graduates possess knowledge, confidence, competencies, and ethical consciousness to assume larger roles of responsibility and leadership as productive citizens prepared to promote the general welfare and serve the community through lifelong learning and scholarship.

Why O.A.S.I.S.?

Why a new academic institution for the Caribbean? The traditional characteristics of education have changed. The natural features of the education landscape seem to change with the daily tide. Procedures and methodology that were taboo yesterday are acceptable or even advanced today. In an era when a student may "earn" an accredited degree without seeing a classroom, a member of the faculty, or another student, little remains sacred in education. The past criticism of the Old World tutorial method has turned into imitation as it is used with new technology to meet the tutoring needs of learners separated from the traditional classroom.

Omega **A**dvanced **S**chools for **I**nterdisciplinary **S**tudies (O.A.S.I.S.) is an outgrowth of the Task Force (1974 - 1981) and more recent information from the Fifth International Conference on Adult Education (Hamburg, Germany, 1997), the conference at the University of Mumbai (India, 1998), and the UNESCO World Conference on Higher Education (Paris, 1998). The recommendations were to open schools, colleges and universities to adult learners and adapt programs and learning conditions to meet adult needs.

The task was to develop coherent mechanisms to recognize the outcomes of learning undertaken in different contexts, bring the services of universities to outside groups and to concentrate on interdisciplinary research in all aspects of adult education and learning with the participation of adult learners themselves. This effort was to include opportunities for adult learning in flexible, open and creative ways, taking into account the different needs of people in a multicultural and pluralistic environment. In considering the difficulty of transforming existing colleges and universities into agencies for lifelong education, it became apparent that a new university structured under new conditions could better meet the needs of the 21st Century. OASIS University grew out of this need recognized by higher educators, scholars and specialists in the area of adult learning and lifelong education.

The leadership of **O**mega **A**dvanced **S**chools for **I**nterdisciplinary **S**tudies (O.A.S.I.S.) was guided by the following essential elements that characterize an institution structured to support lifelong education.

1. **Establish** a bridging framework to provide the contexts to facilitate lifelong learning.
2. **Negotiate** partnerships and strategic linkages with other institutions and groups.
3. **Facilitate** interdisciplinary research.
4. **Develop** a teaching/learning process that permits self-directed learning in real life situations.
5. **Initiate** academic policies and mechanisms to give priority to learning.
6. **Establish** dialog/support systems suitable for adult learners
7. **Strive** for a global strategy with a broad exchange of

teaching/learning systems and collaboration across national boundaries.

O.A.S.I.S. exists because of a Caribbean need and technology. Technological-assisted learning and online learning have made many early tutorial procedures of Old World education a valuable asset to both faculty and student. Technology has changed the face of education forever and made many procedures and processes outmoded. The growth of the Internet and other interactive media systems has permitted an academic institution to go global and literally reach the world with various educational programs. In such an educational climate, it is time for a new institution that maintains a campus environment, preserves the faculty-student relationship, holds students accountable for academic performance, and upholds academic standards in the learning process.

Action Plan

O.A.S.I.S. leadership articulated an Action Plan to advance the mission of the University. The following specified seven basic objectives were established:

Objective One - Structure academic programs to complement but not compete with existing regional educational programs with academic policies and mechanisms to give priority to specialized learning needs of students.
Objective Two - Provide organizational structures, learning resources, technology and processes designed to motivate and engage students in scholarly activity in a program of study and beyond graduation.
 Objective Three - Provide quality programs of study for mature adults that facilitate interdisciplinary study and research to benefit the Caribbean region in particular, but also reflective of global issues.
Objective Four - Partner with business and industry to produce meaningful research and development for the Caribbean Region.
Objective Five - Develop a teaching/learning process that permits self-directed, individualized, face-to-face and distance learning in real life situations with dialog/support systems and technology suitable for mature adults.

Objective Six - Strive for a global strategy for multicultural awareness with a broad exchange of teaching/learning systems and collaboration across national
Objective Seven - Create an educational climate conducive to adult learning that promotes mutual respect and trust among faculty and students.

PostScript Two

The transformational concepts and constructs used to establish Oxford Graduate School/ACRSS and O.A.S.I.S. University are being utilized to meet a need in the Jewish Community:

YESHIVA TORAH INSTITUTE

Tamid Rishonim "Always First"
http://www.aliyahcongregation.com/yeshiva/

Climbing the ladder toward Biblical Judaism...and Taking positive steps to produce Licentiates in Hebrew Studies and Rabbinical Ordination!

Yeshiva Torah Institute offers affordable interdisciplinary study and degree programs to serve the community of Biblical Judaism with interactive residency, distance learning elements and Internet dialog/support designed to facilitate learning through innovative methodology and faculty support.

_____**www.dialyeshiva.net**_____

YESHIVA TORAH INSTITUTE
Monument, Colorado USA
2010

Transformational Leadership in Education

ISBN 978-0-9801674-6-7

GlobalEdAdvancePress™

CPSIA information can be obtained at www.ICGtesting.com
Printed in the USA
LVOW121730050712

288897LV00018B/1/P